Winner
Take
All

ALSO BY DAMBISA MOYO

How the West Was Lost

Dead Aid

Winner
Take
All

CHINA'S RACE FOR RESOURCES

AND WHAT IT MEANS

FOR THE WORLD

Dambisa F. Moyo

BASIC BOOKS

A Member of the Perseus Books Group

Books published by Basic Books are available at special discounts for bulk purchases
in the United States by corporations, institutions, and other organizations. For more
information, please contact the Special Markets Department at the Perseus Books
Group, 2300 Chestnut Street, Suite 200, Philadelphia, PA 19103, or call (800) 810-4145,
ext. 5000, or e-mail special.markets@perseusbooks.com.

Editorial production by Lori Hobkirk at the Book Factory.
DESIGN BY JANE RAESE

A CIP catalog record for this book is available from the Library of Congress.
ISBN 978-0-465-02828-3

10 9 8 7 6 5 4 3 2 1

"If we shrink from the hard contests where men must win at hazard of their lives and at the risk of all they hold dear, then the bolder and stronger peoples will pass us by and will win for themselves the domination of the world."

— THEODORE ROOSEVELT
"The Strenuous Life," 1899

"Always pray that your opposition be wicked. In wickedness there is a strong strain toward rationality . . . If good intentions are combined with stupidity, it is impossible to outthink them."

— MARION J. LEVI JR.
Nine Laws for the Disillusionment of the True Liberal, 1970

Contents

CONTENTS

Winner
Take
All

Introduction

IN THE SUMMER OF 2007 a Chinese company bought a mountain in Peru. More specifically, it bought the mineral rights to mine the resources contained in it. At fifteen thousand feet (forty-six hundred meters), Mount Toromocho is an imposing landmass—more than half the height of Mount Everest. It contains two billion tons of copper, one of the largest single copper deposits in the world. For a hefty fee of US$3 billion, Mount Toromocho's title transferred from the Peruvian people to the hands of the Chinese.

China's commodity campaign is breathtaking. In just over a decade China has risen from relative insignificance to pole position in underwriting numerous resource-related transactions across the globe. China's Chinalco, the company that bought the rights to exploit the Peruvian mountain, also spent nearly US$13 billion in 2008 for a stake in Australia's aluminum sector.[1] In June 2009 Sinopec—a leading Chinese petrochemical company—purchased Addax Petroleum, which has sizeable assets in Iraq and Nigeria, for US$7.2 billion. Sinopec also bought a 40 percent stake in the Brazilian arm of Repsol, a Spanish energy company, for US$7 billion in October 2010 and part ownership in a joint-venture oil company with Russia's Rosneft (a leading oil and gas company) for US$3.5 billion in June 2006.

Collectively, these inputs used to produce goods and services are known as commodities, and commodities permeate every aspect of modern daily living: the energy that powers cars, trucks, and electricity grids; water for the sustenance of all life forms; arable land that yields grains and other foodstuffs; and a long list of minerals used in everything from mobile telephony to television screens and as inputs to all sorts of machinery.

1

Little wonder that headline writers and media commentators telegraph warnings of impending doom in the commodity space—conflicts spurred by shortages of arable land, clashes over water, and the risks of political Armageddon as global demand for energy outstrips supply. Yet for all the importance of commodities and the markets in which they trade, our knowledge of this essential component of the global economy—the largest asset class in the world—remains blurry at best.

Winner Take All explores the commodity dynamics that the world will face over the next several decades that almost certainly will be characterized by global tensions arising from greater resource scarcity. More specifically, it is about the mechanics and implications of China's rush for resources across all regions of the world. Of all the world's great powers, only one, China, has focused its economic and political strategy on anticipating the considerable challenges presented by a resource-scarce future. But more than this, *Winner Take All* is a clarion call to the rest of the world, which remains largely ill prepared for the challenges of resource scarcity and the evolving dynamics around China's central role. This despite the well-reasoned arguments laid out by one of the world's foremost and renowned commodities experts, Jim Rogers, on the importance of resources in his book, *Hot Commodities,* nearly a decade ago.

What is at stake? At a minimum, acute resource scarcity will lead the world into a period when the average prices for commodities—arable land, water, minerals, and oil—will skyrocket to permanently higher levels. Food at supermarkets (bread from wheat and grains as well as sugar, meat, milk, etc.), water from taps, mobile phones and cars, gasoline at the pumps, and many of the other daily costs of life will be substantially higher. And higher prices will, inevitably, lead to worsening living standards across the world.

In the extreme case, as resource scarcity becomes more biting, commodity shortages could lead to outright war. As we discuss later, since 1990 at least eighteen violent conflicts around the world—many of them ongoing—have had their origins in resource shortages and access. Beyond this, numerous other countries in commodity-scarce regions, such as the water-scarce Middle East or parts of Asia with relatively little arable land per person, are vulnerable to violence and clashes. Here and elsewhere populations inhabit a delicate balance between substantial demand and supply shortages. The looming risk, of course, is that many more countries—and thus many more people—will be drawn into the fray.

This is the context in which China's resource campaign is taking place. China's global charge for hard commodities (metals and minerals that are mined or extracted), soft ones (typically grown goods, such as timber, grains, and other foodstuffs), and the infrastructure (roads, ports, and railways) that support and facilitate their extraction and delivery, is meant to guarantee the continuation of its already remarkable story of economic development. To that end, the Chinese appear determined to pull all available levers, and because China's resource undertaking is global and among the most aggressive in history, it has economic consequences for us all.

THIS BOOK TACKLES three broad themes.

First, it examines the *economic* implications of China's ascendancy as the lead buyer of the world's resources, set in the context of global commodity supply and demand. China is now the main trading partner of many of the most influential economies in both the developed and the developing world. In just a few short decades it has become the most sought-after source of capital infusions. Indeed, rich countries and poor alike do not just wait for China to come calling; they actively court and seek out Chinese investments.

China now funds foreign governments (providing loans and buying their bonds), underwrites schools and hospitals, and pays for infrastructure projects such as roads and railways (particularly across the poorest parts of the world), catering to the needs of the host nations and making China an altogether more attractive investor than international bodies such as the World Bank, which often tie loans to harsh policy restrictions. China's economic influence on places as far-flung as the United States, Africa, Eastern Europe, Australia, and South America is incalculable. China's increasing global influence has mirrored its economic rise and, invariably, a concomitant rise in its demand for resources.

Second, this book is about China's growing *financial* reach and its implications for the workings of the global commodity markets. Over time and across the gamut of commodities (minerals and oil markets and even non–publicly traded assets such as land), China has become the marginal buyer, purchasing global resources in such disproportionate volume that it increasingly has price-setting power, which automatically influences how markets trade as well as helping determine the value of assets in host countries. Thus, gleaning the ramifications of China's involvement in setting resource prices and influencing whether market prices move up or down is crucial.

Finally, this book is about the *social* and *political* implications of China's quest for resources. China's role in the world cannot be viewed solely through the narrow prism of economics and finance. Its global campaign not only has serious consequences on geopolitics but also determines how people across the globe live and interact with their governments. China's investments can have a largely positive impact when they help raise per capita incomes and reduce poverty in the host nation, but this newfound wealth can also accrue to despotic governments who use the cash for self-aggrandizement or subjugating the local citizenry. Although the Chinese may not explicitly aim to undermine a host country's political environment, they (as other foreign investors) must carefully balance the benefits of resource investment—creating jobs and laying down infrastructure in countries where such investments are desperately needed—against such political costs.

CHINA IS, OF COURSE, not the first country to launch a global quest for resources. Historical parallels can be seen as far back as the classical Roman campaigns of the first century, in Britain's transcontinental operations at the end of the sixteenth century, and in the rise of modern European and American transnational corporations between the mid-1860s and 1870s. The Industrial Revolution that powered these economies created a voracious demand for raw materials and the need to seek resources far beyond their borders. The European colonization of Africa and the later partitioning of the oil-rich Middle East were both, in essence, commodity grabs. As impressive as its resource campaign is, China appears to aspire to nothing quite so directly territorial. But China does have two tools in its favor that earlier commodity seekers often lacked, at least in similar quantity: vast wealth and vast economic and political discipline.

In a world where cash is king, China's much-noted cash stockpile—over US$3 trillion in foreign currency reserves in 2012—affords it the ability to do what other countries can't do and go where other countries can't go. Simply put, the Chinese are on a global shopping spree. And its voracious commodity appetite is unlikely to abate significantly even if China's economic growth rates were to cool.

Poor countries such as Peru think nothing of mortgaging and selling off their assets, even when those assets come in the form of a fifteen thousand–foot mountain of copper, as they badly need the money to finance economic growth and development. Meanwhile, heavily indebted industrialized countries that need to raise revenues also capitulate, borrowing significant sums from China. In 2011, for example, China was the largest single holder of US government debt, with 26 percent of all foreign-held US Treasury securities (around 8 percent of total US public debt). Increasingly, countries like Japan, South Korea, and others across the Middle East have embarked on their own commodity campaigns—particularly with regard to Africa's arable land—but China's size, cash (i.e., its ability to outbid the competition), and unyielding determination mean, for now, it's mostly all about China.

But who is China? Is it right to combine all of China's parts into one monolithic entity? And is the sum always greater than the constituent parts? China's success relies on many different agents—

individuals, corporations, and the Communist Party state. But ultimately they all pull together—public or private—under one unifying force with a single agenda: the betterment of China.

This philosophy is perhaps best encapsulated in China's "peaceful rise" policy line, popularized in numerous speeches between 1997 and 2004 by Zheng Bijian, a foreign policy spokesman.[2] These speeches, along with the Government Work Report (similar to the US president's State of the Union address) delivered annually by the Chinese premier, have laid out the leadership's strategic aims for the country. From economic growth targets to technology strategy to foreign policy and statements about China's role in the world, these articulations do a good job of stressing the aspirations of China's political class and the important factors integral to development, mainly public goods such as education, health care, and domestic infrastructure.

In principle there is little to distinguish many of these goals from those of other governments. In China's case, however, it's less about these relatively uncontroversial proclamations and more about how China's political infrastructure goes about executing China's agenda. Through a centrally planned command-and-control system of the economy, China's Communist Party sponsors and influences the behavior of mammoth state-owned enterprises such as banks, energy firms, transport and logistic businesses, and resource companies. More generally, the Chinese state's subscription to state-led capitalism (where the government takes a central role in driving profit-making, commercial activities) means that all actors are primarily focused on meeting the goals of the Communist Party, so that even the blind profit-making motives of Chinese businessmen fall behind the Politburo's political desires.

So how does the Chinese government ensure that its philosophy of national purpose prevails? It uses regulation, money, and personnel.

The regulatory process is pretty straightforward. Like other governments around the world, the Chinese government provides the strictures to set up businesses in the form of investment codes, licensing rules, and business-operating guidelines under which individuals and corporations must operate. The business environment is monitored through a web of regulatory bodies such as its central bank and agencies that grant consents or permissions for businesses to operate, among them the State Administration for Industry and Commerce and the Quality and Technology Supervision Bureau.[3] But more than this, the important issue is the reach of the government—how long, exactly, the long arm of the law is. In China's case it's pretty clear that "regulation" goes much further than simply issuing permits and authorizing licenses for businesses to operate.

The Chinese party state also enforces its philosophy of national purpose through money—by controlling the allocation of its vast public funds, including China's foreign reserves. The allocation of China's public purse is guided by at least two factors. First, public proclamations on economic policy imperatives such as those contained in the Government Work Report discussed above as well as statements aimed at those sectors and industries (e.g., food production and energy) feed into China's overarching plans to continue to drive economic growth and reduce poverty. It is high and sustainable growth rates, as well as a continual reduction in poverty, that, above all else, drive the Chinese state actions. Second, China's cash disbursements are influenced by broader market conditions that may warrant that the state step in to boost lackluster economic growth or intervene in times of economic crisis. In November 2008, for example, the government implemented a US$586 billion (around 4 trillion renminbi) stimulus package to combat the ill effects of the financial crisis (rising unemployment led by the shrinking export industry and, thus, a slowdown in economic growth) in a matter of days. China's stimulus package amounted to nearly 15 percent of annual economic output spread over two years.[4]

The government makes its financial muscle felt, so the line between public and private can appear deliberately obfuscated: for example, the Chinese state retains sizeable equity stakes in many publicly traded companies (in some cases upward of 70 percent of these companies are government owned) and virtually all of the top thirty Chinese multinational enterprises are state owned. Often Chinese enterprises investing in strategic sectors such as oil, minerals, or infrastructure are state owned, and thus, in a sense, they act as extensions of the party state. This structure has been central to China's global resource drive. For instance, the three leading investors in Africa are state-owned oil companies: China Petrochemical Corporation, China National Petroleum Corporation, and China National Offshore Oil Corporation.

China's so-called going-out strategy uses state-controlled tools to encourage overseas expansion and acquisitions by even privately held companies. Many Chinese enterprises receive government grants or (low-interest) loans from state-owned banks, placing them at a distinct advantage compared with foreign companies that have to source funds with more expensive borrowing from the financial markets. Numerous Chinese companies benefit not only from concessional credit lines (i.e., credit lines that provide flexible or lenient terms for repayment, generally with extended repayment periods and at lower interest rates than market rates) but also from tax breaks and priority allocation of key contracts. In 2009, for example, Wuhan Iron and Steel, China's third-largest steelmaker, was extended a nearly US$12 billion line of credit by the state-owned China Development Bank. A primary goal of the loan was to finance its "overseas resource base construction," including the roll-out of large iron mines and steel plants that would produce these commodities. Such loans became common as the Chinese government encouraged state-owned banks to lend in order to stimulate the economy in the wake of the 2008 financial crisis.

Finally, China's control is about people and personnel. Roughly 10 percent—nearly eighty million people, and growing—of China's workforce are card-carrying Communist Party members. It's not just the number of party cadres that matters but that party members are almost always strategically placed to ensure that all sectors are infused with the Communist Party's overarching national purpose. It's not unusual for publicly traded enterprises to "employ" party cadres to such an extent that these party representatives are seen as more important, more powerful, and more influential than the CEOs of those nominally independent entities.

In extreme cases companies' senior staff is appointed by the Chinese government and chief executives hold ministerial level rank. And despite being operationally independent, companies are regularly seen to conform and adhere to the Communist Party policy. From the vantage point of the companies, their relationship with the government is a balancing act between the benefits they get, such as concessional funding and international contacts brokered by the Chinese state (e.g., contacts with senior public officials and foreign governments established by the Chinese government) and the costs of government interference and pressures of compliance with the Communist Party's worldview.

The strategy of providing China's network of companies access to (cheap) money and Chinese state endorsements as well as preferential access to foreign government contacts (who themselves are central players in the resource sector in their respective countries) seems to help steer China's developmental agenda. And because this approach works well for the Chinese government and the command-and-control approach of the Communist Party, it is unlikely to change any time soon. If anything, Chinese state interventions would likely increase were the economy to face a "hard landing" that would see a considerable contraction in China's economic growth, as some economists were predicting in 2012.

To many Sinophiles the Chinese government is omnipresent and omnipotent. However, the degree of government influence, one Chinese businessperson quipped, depends on the extent to which you are licensed, take public money, and who you have as (and, relatedly, who selects) your key personnel—such as the CEO, board members, or the chief financial officer. It's the difference between being told explicitly what you should do, where to invest, who to hire, and so on (if you take the license, the money, and the people) versus being told what you should not do—for example, barring a company from investing outside an explicitly stated sector (if you only seek a license). The emergent patterns around deal financing and transactions struck in all areas of natural resources fit snugly into China's imperative for its vast domestic infrastructure build-out and plan for longer-term economic growth. This is China, Inc.—all for one, and one for all.[5]

PART I

China's Rush for Resources

CHAPTER 1

The Drivers of World Commodity Demand

To UNDERSTAND THE EVENTS of the next fifty years one must first and foremost understand environmental scarcity or "diminishing natural resources." So penned Robert Kaplan in 1994 in his article titled "The Coming Anarchy: How Scarcity, Crime, Overpopulation, Tribalism, and Disease Are Rapidly Destroying the Social Fabric of Our Planet." Kaplan offered a chilling vision of the future, foretelling in vivid and painstaking detail how the global scarcity of resources would contribute to worldwide demographic, environmental, and societal stress.

Whether or not we accept Kaplan's dire vision, it is clear that in order to understand China's approach to securing global resources, we must set it in the broader context of the global demand for commodities. Ultimately, global commodity supply also matters (this is discussed in the next two chapters), but this chapter considers the evolving demand dynamics: why global demand pressures across the commodity complex—arable land, water, energy, and minerals—are set to increase, and how these demand factors will exacerbate resource scarcity in the decades to come.

The Malthusian Chronicles

Kaplan's article was not the first to identify a dearth of resources as the catalyst of an impending global cataclysm. As early as 1798 Thomas Malthus in his "Essay on the Principle of Population" argued that population growth generally expands in times and places of plenty, until the size of the population relative to the primary available resources causes distress. In essence, Malthus argued, the limits on the availability of commodities are what keep population growth in check. The Club of Rome's 1972 report "The Limits to Growth" built on Malthusian theory in modeling the impact of a growing world population against finite (and depleting) resource supplies. The Club's conclusion: this supply-versus-demand disequilibrium would constrain economic growth and could consign large swathes of the global population to poverty.

Four decades later commodity imbalances continue apace.

The exponential growth of the world's population and the technology that has accompanied it over the past fifty years have placed unprecedented pressures on commodity demand of all manner of resources—from food and water (itself an input to food) to energy and minerals (as, say, heating and plumbing inputs for a rapidly expanding global population). Even ten years ago few anticipated how many of us would be carrying personal technological devices or the rapidly increasing share of the global population that would be car owners, yet both are a tremendous draw on finite mineral resources.

To be sure, the world economy has largely been bailed out by technological advances that have generated productivity gains, greater efficiencies, and improved utilization of resources. But if they have delayed our day of reckoning, it's far from clear that they will do so forever. As advancements to boost resource supply stall and global commodity demand skyrockets, a scarier picture is emerging, one in which the resources on which we depend today—many of them nonrenewable—are depleting into nonexistence or are so poorly matched that their demand and supply might never be able to meet. Yet, as we highlight throughout this chapter, China seems to be the only country that's preparing for this eventuality in a sustainable and deliberately constructive way, by making friends across the globe and systematically and continually investing across the commodities complex.

Driving Resource Demand

Like virtually all goods and services, commodity prices are driven by supply and demand. As canonical economic models suggest, where these two meet, the price of the commodity is set.

As we shall discuss in subsequent chapters, the factors driving the *supply* of land, water, energy, and minerals are complicated by the fact that there are cross-linkages among the different resources. For example, the supply of food, such as grains and beef, crucially depends on the availability of both arable land and water. So gaining access to these underlying resources matters almost as much as the target commodity itself and ultimately determines the price and availability of the broader spectrum of food products.

In contrast, the factors influencing the *demand* for soft and hard commodities are broadly the same. At a very basic level the two influential factors are population dynamics (the absolute size of the world's population and prospects for global population growth) and the increases in wealth that are driven, in particular, by rapid economic growth in emerging economies. Naturally, the implications of these wealth increases on consumption patterns will be considerable.

The Global Population Grows

In just sixty years the global population has exploded—from around 2.5 billion in 1950 to 7 billion in 2011. The chart below tells the story in shorthand: a gentle slope emerging out of the Middle Ages and Renaissance, a slight rise in the incline around 1928 when the Scottish scientist Alexander Fleming stumbled serendipitously upon penicillin, and then the steep Everest-like slope as medical interventions became ever more sophisticated, infant mortality rates nose-dived, and average life expectancy rose. Demographers now forecast that the world's population will expand by an additional 1.2

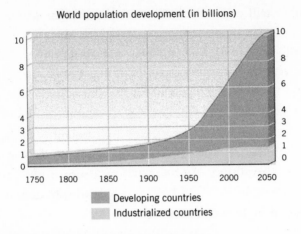

World population development (in billions)

Developing countries
Industrialized countries

Figure 1.1. Skyrocketing World Population

Source: Philippe Rekacewicz, "World Population Development," UNEP/GRID-Arendal, http://www.grida.no/graphicslib/detail/world-population-development_29db\.

billion over the next twenty years, so that by 2050 there will be as many as 10 billion people living on the planet—a 40 percent increase in the world population in a mere forty years.

The good news is that the pace at which the world population is growing will gradually slow, offering a reprieve on commodity demands. The UN expects women almost everywhere to bear fewer children by the middle of the twenty-first century. Currently the global average is 2.6 children per woman, down from 4.3 in the 1970s; this is expected to decline to just 2 by 2050. The bad news is that in the shorter term the pressures exerted on global resources by the prospects of a global population approaching 10 billion are ominous.[1]

To complicate matters further—and the graph also shows this—the greatest population growth is forecast in precisely the regions with the highest prospect for rapid increases in wealth and a concomitant greater demand for resources. According to the US National Intelligence Council publication *Global Trends 2025: A Transformed World,* nearly all of the population growth over the next twenty years will come from Africa, Asia, and Latin America, with less than 3 percent from the developed West. More developed countries like the United States still register population growth, but at a slowing rate. For instance, according to the US Census Bureau, the US population grew by around 2.8 million people between April 2010 and July 2011, from both immigration and increased births.

However, it's not just that there will be more people on the planet. The global population in its entirety is getting wealthier, and it is this newfound wealth that could put pressure on resource demand and ultimately wreak havoc on the supply-demand balance across the commodity complex.

The World's Population Gets Wealthier

In 2001 Goldman Sachs economists came up with an acronym to capture what they saw as the amazing economic growth prospects of the leading emerging economies—Brazil, Russia, India, and China, known as BRICs. Their now well-known BRIC estimates projected that by 2050 these countries would be four of the top five largest economies in the world.

The following year, in 2002, Goldman Sachs calculated that the increase in China's dollar GDP had been effectively the same as creating two new Indias, a new Italy, and nearly a new France or UK. The economists at Goldman Sachs have since revised their estimates upward as the BRICs have posted greater economic gains in a shorter period of time than originally expected. By 2010, for example, China's GDP had grown by almost US$4 trillion since 2000—meaning China has, in fact, created another seven Indias (at its 2001 size), nearly three Italys, and more than two Frances. Simply put, more economic growth means more wealth means more commodity demand.

In the past two decades China has had the world's fastest-growing economy, overtaking Japan to become the world's number-two economy after the United States in 2010. If China continues on this trajectory, it is poised to become the world's biggest economy by 2025. But even if it hits a temporary roadblock, the fundamental path of economic improvement points to only higher levels of commodity demand, even if at a slower rate of change. The tremendous economic progress around the world and the global wealth that it has unleashed has far-reaching and untold effects on the global demand for commodities. A richer average population will demand more and better quality foodstuffs, goods, and services—all of which require more resources.

If China is this century's biggest growth story, it is not the only one. India—home to some 1.2 billion people, around 17 percent of the global population—has followed closely behind China in this relentless economic march forward. Conservative estimates put the Indian subcontinent's growth rate over the last several decades at an average of nearly 5 percent a year, lower than China's at 7.5 percent, but still impressive—and remarkably consistent. All told, the combined GDP of the BRIC countries is thought to have risen from US$2.5 trillion at the beginning of 2000 to close to US$9 trillion by 2010. (By comparison, the United States is thought to have added US$4.5 trillion over the same period.) This continuing economic growth across the emerging world—not just among the BRICs—has led forecasters to predict that by 2030 at least 2 billion new people will join the global middle class. Put another way, in less than twenty years we will witness the creation of a middle class of roughly the same size as the current total population of Africa, North America, and Europe.

At one level this is a global success story of remarkable proportions. By the mid-2020s over 200 million people in the BRICs could have incomes over US$15,000. To people living in developed economies this might not seem like much—in the United States, for example, per capita incomes are around US$47,000—but given that many emerging economies had average incomes of around US$1,000 thirty years ago, such income forecasts are astounding.[2] The tremendous economic progress around the world is, however, a mixed blessing. A richer average populous is certain to demand more and better quality goods and services, all of which require more resources. A small example of how the voracious appetite for commodities of all kinds will expand are forecasts that global demand for food and water will increase by 50 and 30 percent respectively by 2030.

Planes, Trains, and Automobiles

Microdata confirm that the phenomenon of rapidly increasing economic wealth is not just a macroeconomic occurrence. At the end of 2008, for example, China recorded more dollar millionaires than the UK—364,000 versus 362,000 respectively. India—still regarded in many Western eyes as a poor country—has an estimated US$500 billion in private money abroad. Aside from boasting the world's largest middle class, numbering some 450 million people, India is also home to at least fifty native-grown billionaires.

In less than half a century China alone has managed to transform the livelihoods of some three hundred million of its people, shifting them from abject poverty to economic standards that rival the West—a feat unprecedented in the history of the world. India's aggregate poverty ratio (defined as the percent of people living on less than US$1.25 a day) has shifted from nearly 60 percent in 1981 to just over 40 percent in 2005. Over the same period China's poverty statistics have gone from 85 percent to 16 percent. (The closest comparable statistic in the United States has hovered around 15 percent in the same time frame.[3])

Both China and India have accomplished amazing feats in improving living standards for their citizens, but such massive increases in wealth and economic power invariably come with increases in demand—for virtually everything. As incomes rise, so does the demand for more protein-based foods like meats and chicken (a substitution pattern in which people replace cheaper wheat and root-based foods like potatoes with more expensive and protein-rich meats[4]); better-quality housing with indoor heating, water, and plumbing; and more efficient transportation and telecommunications in the form of cars and telephones.

By 2010 rapidly emerging economies were already registering double-digit growth in domestic demand—15 percent in China and 10 percent in both India and Brazil—fuelled in large part by demand pressures from their newly arriving and voracious consumers. And China alone ranked first in demand for mobile phones and cars, and second in electricity consumption.

Each of these creature comforts requires commodity inputs—such as metals like copper, gold, lead, nickel, palladium, and aluminum used in the production of the frames, batteries, and circuit boards of computers or mobile phones. To place this demand in context, as of 2010 an estimated 5.3 billion mobile phones were in use worldwide, accounting for approximately 77 percent of the world's population and fast approaching one cell phone for every man, woman, or child on the planet today.

What does that mean in terms of commodities and resources? A July 2006 fact sheet titled "Recycled Cell Phone—A Treasure Trove of Valuable Metals," compiled by the US Geological Survey, is revealing. It provided separate breakdowns for the 180 million cell phones then in use in the United States, another 130 million expected to be retired that year, and the 500 million obsolete cell phones sitting in drawers and closets awaiting disposal. In the aggregate, as shown in the table below, those 810 million cell phones contained over thirteen thousand metric tons of metals, with a collective net worth of more than half a billion US dollars. To put it more graphically, the sum total of all phones in use, retired, and out of circulation in the United States in 2005 was equivalent to the amount of metal contained in fifty 747 jumbo jets.[5] And this is just the United States in just one year at a time when cell phones were in their relative infancy.

One estimate holds that there are now over 327 million cell phones in use in the United States alone—that is, over one phone for each person in the population. China and India, amongst the

Table 1.1. The weight and value of metal in US cell phones, 2005

Metal	Metal content for 810 million cell phones in use, retired, or obsolete and awaiting disposal, in metric tons	Value of 810 million cell phones in use, retired, or obsolete and awaiting disposal, in US dollars
Copper	12,900.0	$27.8 million
Silver	288.1	$49.9 million
Gold	27.1	$323.0 million
Palladium	12.1	$101.7 million
Platinum	0.28	$6.3 million
Total	13,227.58	$508.7 million

Source: Adapted from: US Geological Survey (USGS), "Recycled Cell Phones—A Treasure Trove of Valuable Metals," July 2006, http://pubs.usgs.gov/fs/2006/3097/fs2006-3097.pdf.

most rapidly growing economies in the world, together have nearly two billion cell phones in use, close to a billion in China alone. Odds are that both these nations will soon converge to mobile-phone penetration rates similar to or greater than the United States. Add to that the demand pressures from the soaring use of other mobile electronics—iPads, Kindles, laptops, and the like—and it's easy to see that the demand pressure on metals like copper, gold, and palladium will continue to mount ever higher in the decade ahead.

Meanwhile cars, light trucks, and the automobile industry as a whole also absorb huge quantities of metals. A typical auto draws not only on plastics (for the dashboard and cupholder), leather for the seats, glass for the windows, and rubber for the tires, but also a number of metals and minerals. According to the World Steel Association, roughly 55 percent of a car's weight comes from steel—roughly two thousand four hundred pounds of steel per standard auto or three thousand pounds in the average SUV or light truck. Aluminum ranks second among auto metals, accounting for about three hundred pounds in the average North American vehicle. Add to that copper (the London Metal Exchange estimates 7 percent of copper consumption is linked to the transportation industry), platinum (60 percent of platinum is used in the auto industry), palladium, rhodium, lead (primarily used in batteries), tin (used in solders to fuse different metal pieces), cobalt (in airbags), and zinc (used in engineering to galvanize metals and protect cars from the elements), and a car begins to resemble a mining product as much as it does a manufacturing one.

Automobiles are, in fact, aggregates of processed commodities—and thus also resource depletions—and although the car market has sagged generally with the global economy in recent years, they remain hugely in demand in the fastest-growing markets. Since 2004 unit car sales in China have grown at an average annual rate of over 20 percent; Beijing, China's administrative capital, sees around two thousand additional cars come onto its streets every day. In all, China is expected to account for about 60 percent of all auto sales to the BRIC nations in the years immediately ahead, but sales growth should be brisk in Russia, India, and Brazil as well. A Boston Consulting Group report estimates that total auto purchases across all four BRICs will account for about 30 percent of global sales by 2014.

As much as it exacerbates metals and mineral depletion, rising demand for middle-class preferences also means pressure for oil and energy. Somewhere over one billion people traveled on airplanes in 2011, making fifty thousand flights a day, or roughly eighteen million flights a year. And these estimates are for commercial flights only: private jets and military aircraft usage is not included. If you consider that a Boeing 747-400 ER jet, on average, burns through five gallons (nineteen liters) of oil per mile, the impact on global oil supplies of hundreds of thousands of miles covered on millions of flights is enormous. Consider, for example, this one data point: the Singapore to Newark, New Jersey, route is the longest commercial travel route: an approximately ten-thousand-mile (sixteen thousand kilometers) journey that lasts roughly nineteen hours. At five gallons a mile, the aircraft needs fifty thousand gallons to go the distance—one way. Again increasing demand on the world's resources.

Throughout the book we will continue to look at how other resources (land, water, energy) seep into our day-to-day living, but suffice it to say, with the population and wealth dynamics at play, the demand for natural resources around the world will continue to rise dramatically.

An Urban Wave

Income growth impacts commodities indirectly too by spurring urbanization. The relative prosperity of cities attracts wave after wave of migrants from rural areas. Significantly greater prospects for employment (e.g., in manufacturing or construction, as opposed to tilling the land in subsistence agriculture) and better quality of life (indoor plumbing and sanitation, televisions, washing machines, and electricity) are a huge draw. The knock-on effects on commodity demand are clearly evident: more consumer goods and better living standards directly translate into more demand for resources.

In the "State of the World Population 2007: Unleashing the Potential of Urban Growth," the UN Population Fund noted that "in 2008, the world reaches an invisible but momentous milestone: For the first time in history, more than half its human population, 3.3 billion people, will be living in urban areas. By 2030, this is expected to swell to almost 5 billion." Much of this urban shift will be felt across the developing world, whose cities and towns will make up 81 percent of urbanites by 2030.

In the poorest regions of the world—Africa and Asia (despite marked improvements in aggregate wealth, there remain enormous pockets of poverty across Asia)—urban populations will double between 2000 and 2030. This is equal to the accumulated urban growth of these two regions during the whole span of history—duplicated in a single generation! To put a finer point to the matter, over the twentieth century the world's urban population grew from around 220 million to 2.8 billion—an eleven-fold rise (or an over 1,000 percent increase). Today, globally, the world is adding people to urban areas at the rate of 60 million each month.

It's All About China

China's pursuit of global commodities is spurred by its seemingly insatiable demand for the array of resources needed to drive economic growth and reduce poverty. And given China's sheer size, what happens in China has broad implications for the path of global resource demand more generally.

Although it is true that population dynamics and unprecedented wealth increases are not the sole domain of China (other economies across South America, Africa, and Asia are meaningfully adding to the world's middle class and, thus, demand-pressure for commodities), China stands apart in the scale of its demand and its very deliberate plan to search for global resources. For instance, combined/aggregated statistics mask the salient point that China's urbanization path is more aggressive and more rapid than in most other countries.

Take India, for example, home to the world's fastest-growing urban populations. In 1950 17 percent of India's population lived in cities, compared to only 13 percent in China. Between 1950 and 2005, however, China urbanized significantly more rapidly than India, ending up with urbanization rates of 41 percent and 29 percent, respectively. This trend is set to continue.

Looking to the future, the McKinsey Global Institute forecasts that China will add 400 million people to its urban population by 2025, so that urbanites will account for 64 percent of China's total population; in India urban rates will soar to 38 percent of its population as 215 million people move to the cities. Meanwhile, over just one decade (between 2008 and 2018) the number of new urban residents is projected to increase to at least 160 million in China, compared to 100 million in India, 50 million in Indonesia, and around 20 million in Brazil and Nigeria.

In 2010 China already had forty cities with populations of a million people or more. By 2020 it plans to add around 225 fully functioning new cities, each to be inhabited by at least one million people. This is part of a government-sponsored phased migration program that will see many more Chinese move from the rural outskirts to urban areas in a much more orderly and systematic way. China already has plans to roll out roughly 170 new mass transportation systems in the next several decades, linking the vast landscape vertically and horizontally and enabling the mass movement of people and goods across a vast network. The implications for commodity demand to support this urban infrastructure are tremendous.[6]

From Demand to Supply

China has nothing if not lofty ambitions, and these are what fuel its rampage on global resources. To meet this challenge, China has already, between 2005 and 2011, engaged in over 350 foreign direct investments valued at more than US$400 billion, much of which is in natural resources. To put this in perspective, for those three hundred weeks (the six-year period) Chinese spending averaged US$1 billion per week (more on this later). If China's strategy comes to fruition, its execution will require a lot of arable land, a lot of usable water, a lot of energy, and a lot of minerals.

However, though critical, taken in isolation, demand dynamics are only half of the equation. The risk is that commodity demand will expand more quickly than the world supply can accommodate. The inevitable result would be recurring shortages of key materials, and it is these shortages that could foment global conflicts. If global supply of the full spectrum of resources can keep up with projected increases in demand, there is not much to fret about. But if commodity supply can't meet demand, then the imbalances place the global economy as a whole on a precarious path. So where does the world stand on the supply side of natural resources?

As noted earlier, the factors driving commodity demand are in a sense universal, impacting all commodities—land, water, energy, and minerals. However, given the distinctive nature of each of these resources—for instance, their sources, whether they can be moved, the ease of trading, and their uses—their supply dynamics are necessarily unique. Thus, the issues governing each must also be individual in nature.

However, as we shall see, the world's most important commodities have one crucial thing in common: they are increasingly becoming scarce, as the earth's (finite) natural resources supply has not adequately kept up with the rising demand. China continues to play a central role in placing inordinate demand on the world's finite supply as well as a central role in gaining access to the flow of the full range of commodities. To set China's approach in context, the following two chapters focus precisely on the special factors influencing the supply of land and water and oil, gas, and minerals, providing a snapshot of the global supply of each resource.

CHAPTER 2

The Resource State of Play: Land and Water

IN FEBRUARY 2011 Zhou Shengxian, China's environment minister, acknowledged publicly that "the depletion, deterioration and exhaustion of resources and the deterioration of the environment have become serious bottlenecks constraining economic and social development."

The Chinese minister's alarm will have certainly been borne of a thorough appraisal of the world supplies of the most important resources—arable land, water, energy, and minerals. In order to see what he saw, a similar-style global stocktaking is crucial. Having analyzed the dynamics driving global commodity demand in the previous chapter, this chapter is our first foray into understanding the state of global resource supply.

More specifically, this chapter (on arable land and water) and the next chapter (on energy and minerals) provide a snapshot of the world's resource supply, and detail where the most important resources lie and in what quantities. Of course, the global resource landscape state is constantly in flux, evolving, and dynamic due to both natural (depletion effects) and man-made interventions (such as mining, tilling land, and extraction). Nevertheless, such an exercise does set in context the supply pressures the world faces and, as we discuss later, defines China's very deliberate and systematic approach to securing global commodities.

Let's begin by taking stock of land.

Terra Firma

Over 29 percent of the earth's surface is composed of dry land, with the remaining 71 percent under water. Land measures approximately 13 billion hectares, or an area about sixteen times the size of the United States. Of that, just 11 percent (or 1.4 billion hectares) is arable—that is, suitable for crops. The other 89 percent—including mountains and deserts—is often prohibitively harder to exploit for food production.

Geographical determinists like Jared Diamond have argued that a country's wealth depends on its environment and topography—in essence, the land. The fact that certain environments are easier to manipulate than others and that those societies that can domesticate plants and animals with relative ease are likely to be more prosperous than those that cannot places an inherent value on land. A country's climate, location, flora, fauna, and terrain all affect the ability of people to provide food for consumption and sustenance, and this ultimately impacts a country's economic growth.

Can the available land adequately support the world's population in the years to come? Population density—the number of people per unit of area of land—is a less useful measure than the density of people per unit of *arable* land.[1] For instance, with the current world population of roughly seven billion, 1.4 billion hectares of arable land means that if land were evenly distributed, every five people would share a hectare (or ten thousand square meters) of land, equivalent to roughly two American football fields. Stretch the global population out to nine billion by 2050, as many forecasts do, and now six people will be sharing a hectare. Clearly, at some point this becomes an end game.

In reality, of course, things don't work out this smoothly. The world's population is anything but evenly distributed. Some countries have a lot of arable land to dedicate to food production, whereas other countries have relatively less. Despite having the world's largest population, China has only around 12 percent arable land, and India, with roughly the same population, has over 50 percent arable land.

The ratio of arable land to population density is not the sole determinant of a nation's capacity to feed its people. Land use and the underlying quality of the arable soil play an important role too. China's use of its arable land as a source of food competes directly with its use as a place where people and government choose to establish homes and cities.

Between 1997 and 2008 the area of arable farmland in China fell by 12.31 million hectares—that is, a loss of around 1 million hectares per year—much of it attributed to the growth in urban centers. Other studies have found that as much as one-sixth of China's arable land is polluted by heavy metals and erosion, whereas desertification has left more than 40 percent of the nation's land degenerated. All in all, this is not a happy picture. Less available land equals less domestic food production, and this equals significant food demand pressures. This is why China has embarked on aggressive land purchase and lease schemes well beyond its borders, particularly in fertile lands in Africa and South America.

The two tables that follow depict the skew in the global supply in arable land. Although Asia and Europe have the largest amount of arable land, they also have the highest population densities, at 200 and 130 people, respectively. On a relative basis this means that there is less arable land available for growing crops and agricultural produce as well as animal husbandry than in, say, Africa, where nearly 8 percent of land is arable and population density is comparatively low, at around 60; South America, with around 7 percent arable land and a population density of 70; North America, with 11 percent arable land and a population density of only 30; or Oceania (Australia and New Zealand), with 6 percent arable land and a population density of just 10 people per square mile.

These statistics would suggest that China should look to North America and, particularly, the United States, with almost as much arable land as China and Brazil combined, to help fulfill its food

Table 2.1. Arable land by region

Region	Arable land (1,000 ha)	Percent of total land area	Population per square mile
Asia	473,206	15.3	200
Europe	277,971	12.6	130
Africa	224,418	7.6	60
North America	207,855	11.1	30
Latin America and the Caribbean	149,602	7.4	70
Oceania	48,154	5.7	10

Source: FAOSTAT Land Use Database, http://faostat.fao.org.

Table 2.2. Arable land: Top-ten countries

Country	Arable land (1,000 ha)	Percent of total land area
United States	162,751	17.8
India	157,923	53.1
Russia	121,750	7.4
China	109,999	11.8
Brazil	61,200	7.2
Australia	47,161	6.1
Canada	45,100	5.0
Nigeria	34,000	37.3
Ukraine	32,478	56.1
Argentina	31,000	11.3

Source: FAOSTAT Land Use Database, http://faostat.fao.org.

needs, and to an extent, that has been the case. In 2010 China surpassed Canada to become the number-one export destination for US agricultural and food produce; soybeans alone accounted for more than half of the nearly US$18 billion in US-China agricultural exports, followed by cotton, animal feeds, and hides. But China neither wants to become beholden to America for its food sustenance nor do Chinese leaders believe that they can meet food needs solely through imports. The Chinese are looking for land abroad on which to grow their own crops, and here North America and the United

States present problems, especially when it comes to land owner-ship and property rights.

Property rights endow a government, corporation, or individual with the exclusive right to determine how a resource is utilized; by extension land rights pertain to the use of land. According to the 2011 International Property Rights Index, the existence of property and land rights across South America and Africa is markedly low. Specif-ically, over 60 percent of the countries ranked in the fourth quintile or bottom 20 percent are in Africa or South America, compared to the United States, which ranked in the top 20 percent in the world.

More simply put, a lot of land across developed economies such as the United States is already spoken for, with access and owner-ship held in private hands. In less developed regions like Africa and South America, however, land ownership largely remains concen-trated in the hands of the state. The state plays a central role in parceling out and granting access, often as lease-holds (where land "ownership" is granted for a specified period of time, and reverts to the owner—in this case, government—when the lease expires) rather than freehold terms (which grant free and unencumbered land ownership rights to the holder), to parties that desire land ac-cess. There are, of course, privately held farms in poorer economies, but the relatively low per capita income levels mean that land own-ership tends to be concentrated in the hands of the wealthy few. All in all, it is far easier for China—and other countries—to negotiate terms (tenure, investment amounts, etc.) for access to significant swathes of arable land with one controlling host entity (in the form of the host government) than numerous small/individual owners.

But there is more. A 2009 joint report of the OECD and the UN Food and Agricultural Organization (FAO) estimates that only 32.5 percent of arable land across the world was actually in productive use, with much of the rest lying fallow.[2] Only 48 percent of potential arable land in China itself is in use. The United States, which for all intents and purposes is food self-sufficient, has only 53 percent of its potential arable land in use. But in both the United States and China this unused arable land has often been effectively claimed by other uses such as urbanization. The real prize here is the continent with the weakest infrastructure or property rights: Africa, home to fully one-third of the earth's remaining untilled arable land.

Logically, then, one might expect Beijing to be looking toward Africa as a kind of subsidiary food basket for the Chinese people, and to an extent that is happening, with recorded Chinese land deals in a range of African countries—from Democratic Republic of Congo to Mozambique, Tanzania, Zambia, and Zimbabwe. For completeness, however, it is worth stressing that the land grab is not just the domain of China.

In its publication "The New Colonialism: Foreign Investors Snap Up African Farmland," *Der Spiegel* highlights multiple instances of relatively richer nations locking in growing rights in poorer countries. The Sudanese government, for instance, has leased 1.5 million hectares of prime farmland to the Gulf States, Egypt, and South Korea for ninety-nine years. Egypt plans to grow wheat and corn on 840,000 hectares in Uganda. And beyond Africa Kuwait has leased 130,000 hectares of rice fields in Cambodia. In a similar vein the South Korean conglomerate Daewoo struck a deal with the government of Madagascar, an island off the east coast of Africa, that would have granted Daewoo full access and a ninety-nine-year lease to a tract of undeveloped land half the size of Belgium. Under the specs of the plan Daewoo was going to utilize 75 percent of the acreage to grow corn and the remainder to grow palm oil, but subsequent political unrest scotched the deal ultimately. China's effort during the 2007 global food crisis to lease 2.5 million acres of the Philippines—to grow crops that would be sent home—also succumbed to local political pressure, but the chase goes on.

Land Registry

The land deals being struck are not just government-to-government trades. Corporations, private individuals, and investment funds of all types and from all over the world are accessing land and staking claims. Given the vast amount of untilled arable land in Africa, governments like China, South Korea, Japan, Qatar, Saudi Arabia, and Kuwait are investing and accessing land all over the continent—all hoping to gain access to this valuable asset. Financial investors and funds have gotten into the act too, betting on global food pressures to drive up the price of land, grains, and other soft commodities required to feed billions of people and satiate demand.

The global land competition is not just about food security either. In fact, a large proportion of the land deals involve crops grown for uses other than food. Increasingly land leases are also being negotiated to produce biofuels and ethanol products meant as alternatives to oil. This puts food and energy in direct competition, given that the grain required to fill a twenty-five-gallon (ninety-five-liter) fuel tank with ethanol could instead feed one person for an entire year.

As World Bank president Robert Zoellick has put it, "While many worry about filling their gas tanks, many others around the world are struggling to fill their stomachs. And it's getting more and more difficult every day." The demand for fuel in rich countries is now seen as competing directly for food in poor countries. In the short term this trade-off worsens the global food supply picture, and over the long term it exacerbates food shortages, which contribute to more hunger and forces the price of food higher. But so long as farmers—particularly farmers in poorer countries struggling to eke out a living—can make more money by switching out of food production to biofuels, they probably will. And so long as they do that, total global food sources will continue to shrink relative to a growing global population.

In a world of finite arable land, anything that detracts from food production points naturally to one direction for food prices—up. Having now conducted a due diligence of the global stock of arable land, we now embark on a similar exercise to glean the worldwide supply of another commodity—water. Bearing in mind that water challenges are, as we shall see, at the center of China's resource woes.

Tapped Out: The Prospects for Water

Land and water go hand in hand. Or they don't. When the former is the case—when arable land is plentiful and water is sufficient to keep the crops growing, the animals watered, power flowing, and production chugging along (water has many uses in modern society), life is good. When arable land is insufficient, governments have to go shopping for other sources of food sustenance, either as agricultural imports or as foreign staging grounds for domestic agriculture. When water is insufficient, the stakes are higher still, because water, unlike food, is not easily transportable, yet it is the basis of the sustenance of life.

In theory, water should never be lacking. Water covers approximately 71 percent of the earth's surface; however, 97 percent of it is too salty for productive use. Of the 2.5 percent that is usable freshwater, 70 percent is in icecaps, and much of the rest is in the ground. This leaves just 0.007 percent of the earth's water supply in the form of readily accessible freshwater, and like arable land, that freshwater is not evenly distributed.

The tables opposite show the distribution of water by region and by country.

Although at first glance China looks like it has reasonably sizeable "home" access to renewable water sources, in practice many of its water sources are contaminated and not safe for human uses.[3] Thus, a large part of China's resource rush relates to efforts to secure access to water for its population. As we shall see, this includes not only investments in cutting-edge technologies (e.g., desalination) but also more aggressive strategies such as rerouting whole rivers.

China's sizeable population means water is not easily or evenly accessible by large proportions of the Chinese citizenry, meaning China's water woes are exacerbated by the fact that the country has too much water where water is not needed and not enough water where it is needed. Ideally water should flow north and east, but many of China's most significant water systems flow south (e.g., the

Table 2.3. Water pooled by region

Region	Total renewable water resources (10^9 m^3/yr)
Latin America and Caribbean	24,039
Asia	15,202
Europe	7,572
North America	6,428
Africa	5,557
Oceania	892

Source: AQUASTAT Database Query, http://www.fao.org/nr/water/aquastat/data/query/index.html.

Table 2.4. Water pooled by country, top ten

Country	Total renewable water resources (10^9 m^3/yr)
Brazil	8,233
Russia	4,508
United States	3,069
Canada	2,902
China	2,840
Colombia	2,132
Indonesia	2,019
Peru	1,913
India	1,911
Democratic Republic of the Congo	1,283

Source: AQUASTAT Database Query, http://www.fao.org/nr/water/aquastat/data/query/index.html.

Mekong River), and many of its important reservoirs are further west than the eastern part of the country, where many millions of China's population congregate. For instance, although the Three Gorges dam is close to Chongqing (by some estimates China's third-most populous city after Shanghai and Beijing) and many other major cities on the Yangtze River, it is a significant distance from the more populous Shanghai on China's eastern border.

The result of these issues is that China's water problem is acute, and its dire water outlook is worsened by the fact that China's total freshwater resources have shrunk by 13 percent since the start of

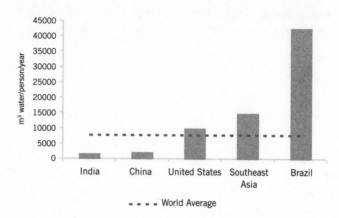

Figure 2.1. Who has water? And who doesn't?

Source: Aquastat, http://www.fao.org/nr/water/aquastat/main/index.stm. Chart design after Agora Financial 2009.

the century. Moreover, as with arable land, a more useful measure is water per person, and by this measure, as seen above, China could be facing a grim future.

Water is officially a "renewable resource"—rainfall, snow melt, and the like "renew" water supplies lost to agriculture and other uses—but the reality is that the total available freshwater supply from existing sources remains largely a constant while the global demand for water rises in direct proportion to a growing global population. Again, to put the matter in simple terms, the Nile River in Africa has an average daily discharge of about three hundred million cubic meters a day. That remains the same whether the Nile is providing the water needs of a million people, ten million, or fifty million, but the cubic meters per day per person changes dramatically as the relevant population rises and its water demand changes over time.

Forecasts suggest that in forty years the global demand for water could exhaust the world's available supply. Already there are indications enough to cause alarm. In 1990 twenty-eight countries with a combined population of 335 million faced chronic water stress or scarcity; a situation in which the demand for potable water exceeds its supply. At the extreme, water scarcity leads to drought, disease, and even death if people (animals and plants also) do not have access to the bare minimum water for sustenance. Such a state is not so rare in the emerging world, where people are often forced to consume contaminated water, leading to such water-borne diseases as cholera and bilharzia, which, if left untreated, can lead to death. By 2025 fifty-two countries covering over 3 billion people, or 40 percent of the world's projected population, are expected to face water shortages. According to *Nature*, an interdisciplinary science journal, in 2010 already 80 percent of the world's population lives in areas with threats to water security.

Climate change also stands to affect water supplies in unpredictable ways. Yes, higher average temperatures on the earth should increase evaporation and generate more rainfall, particularly in areas proximate to rivers, lakes, oceans, and other bodies of water. However, a warming planet might well have an opposite impact on areas further away from water, causing droughts, expanding deserts, and reducing water levels over time—all deleterious for a growing world population with ever-growing water demands.

Water supplies are further complicated by the fact that they frequently spill over political boundaries, forcing multiple countries to share what are often limited (and shrinking) resources. Water supplies are prospectively insufficient along the Nile, directly impacting Egypt, Sudan, and Ethiopia—just as they are from the Euphrates, from which Iraq, Syria, and Turkey draw water. Then, of course, there are the countries dependent on the Jordan River valley—such as, Israel, Jordan, and Syria. (Some estimates suggest that Jordan and Yemen already withdraw 30 percent more water from sources every year than is replenished.)

All this increases the likelihood that the water conflicts of the future will draw in more than one competitor and thus become even more politically challenging if not intractable to solve. And long-standing regional hostilities are virtually certain to exacerbate water-related clashes and hinder efforts to manage the problem effectively. So for example, the long-standing fractious relationship between India and Pakistan will certainly influence the prospects for civility around accessing the Indus waters. Even where water-share agreements do exist, the challenge is to be able to enforce and respect the terms when water scarcity is at its highest.

Yet another factor powerfully drives water supplies: the uses to which the water is put. A relatively primitive culture that lives on nuts, berries, and wild game and warms itself with wood fires needs no more water than is necessary to sustain human life. A society that aspires to more inevitably uses more water, and here China's rapid progression toward economically developed world living standards comes into direct conflict with its limited per capita water supplies.

Globally, around 70 percent of water is used in agriculture, though the percentage is much higher in poorer economies such as those in Africa, where water for agricultural usage is around 86 percent, and Asia, where it is around 81 percent. Worldwide about 20 percent of water goes to industrial purposes, a number that rises considerably in Europe (53 percent) and North America (48 percent). The remaining water—10 percent—is utilized for domestic and primarily urban ends such as sanitation.

Water is linked to food, manufacturing, and energy, where it plays a central role in the creation of electrical and nuclear power. Indeed, even beyond its direct use for sustaining life, water permeates virtually every commodity as an input.

Every time we eat a loaf of bread or consume a steak, we indirectly consume extraordinary quantities of water. In fact, as more food is produced, less water is available for other uses. In "Ecological Integrity: Integrating Environment, Conservation, and Health," David Pimentel, Laura Westra, and Reed F. Noss present figures on how much water it takes to produce various foodstuffs (metric conversions are in parentheses):

Potatoes: 60 gallons of water per pound (or 547 liters a kilogram)
Wheat: 108 gallons per pound (or 986 liters a kilogram)

Corn: 168 gallons per pound (or 1,534 liters a kilogram)
Rice: 229 gallons per pound (or 2,091 liters a kilogram)
Soybeans: 240 gallons per pound (or 2,191 liters a kilogram)
Beef: 12,009 gallons per pound (or 109,671 liters a kilogram)

For a typical American home's serving of food, for example, a breakfast of a couple of eggs (one egg is 62.7 gallons), two slices of white bread (10.6 gallons each), and an eight-ounce cup of milk (worth 48.3 gallons) will use up around 195 gallons of water. A lunch of a four-ounce beef hamburger (615.9 gallons) with one ounce of cheese (56 gallons), and a cup of orange juice (49.1 gallons per cup), uses up 721 gallons of water. And if you eat a two-ounce portion of pasta at dinner, this would use up to 35 gallons of water, so your sum total of water consumption from food (apart from water used for drinking, bathing, sanitation, or washing) for the day is 951 gallons—just for one person, just for one day.

According to the UN, the annual recommended requirement of water per person is between 5,000 gallons and 10,000 gallons. Based on basic food consumption of typical home servings above, it would take a little over five days—less than a week—for an individual American to eat through their minimum water requirements for the year (i.e., 5,000 gallons divided by 951 gallons, which equals 5.26 days). Furthermore, in just over one month (approximately 35 days) the individual would have gone through his or her maximum *annual* water allotment. Food is only one "invisible" drawdown on water; electricity is another.

How much water does it take to make electricity? A 2008 study by the Virginia Water Resources Research Center, a US government–funded institute, revealed the amount of water required to create the energy to power one home in the United States for one month. The results are detailed in Table 2.5.

According to this analysis, it takes 38 liters of water to extract and generate enough natural gas to power a house for one month— that is, to generate 1,000 kilowatt-hours of electricity. To get the

Table 2.5. The amount of water needed to power one US home for one month

Fuel source	Efficiency (liters per 1,000 kilowatt hours)
Natural gas	38
Synfuel: coal gasification	144–340
Tar sands	190–490
Oil shale	260–640
Synfuel: Fisher-Tropsch	530–775
Coal	530–2,100
Hydrogen	1,850–3,100
Liquid natural gas	1,875
Petroleum/oil-electric	15,500–31,200
Fuel ethanol	32,400–375,900
Biodiesel	180,000–969,000

Source: Willie D. Jones, "How Much Water Does It Take to Make Electricity?" IEEE Spectrum, April 2008, http://spectrum.ieee.org/energy/environment/how-much -water-does-it-take-to-make-electricity.

same amount of electricity using a coal source, you will need at least 530 liters of water, and you'll consume as many as 31,200 liters of water if you use petroleum/oil-electric sources.

Biodiesel, most commonly derived in the United States from soybean oil, is often hailed as a sustainable, clean, and more efficient way of generating power. Yet to grow the soybeans, irrigate the soil, and convert them into biodiesel fuel requires at least 180,000 liters of water, enough to power a US house for a month. Over time, as the world faces water shortages and dwindling supplies of energy sources, the average consumer is likely to bear the brunt of these hidden higher water costs, which will be embedded into the price at the pump and higher electricity tariffs.

Whatever the power source, though, whatever the dietary choices, the bottom line for China is that elevated living standards and elevated water use go mostly hand in hand. The economic miracle of modern China certainly can afford the former. The latter, though, is a far more thorny question.

It's All About China

In 2030 China's water demand is expected to reach 216 trillion gallons, but its current supply amounts to just over 163 trillion. The numbers are large and hence can be hard to grasp, but the imbalance between supply and demand is stark. As noted earlier by Chinese minister Zhou Shengxian, water scarcity and chronic stress will continue to make it difficult to expand agricultural production to keep pace with population growth and sustain China's economy.

China's water picture is made worse by factors such as drought and the depletion of water levels, both environmental and manmade. For example, the Yellow and Yangtze rivers as well as their main tributaries are dry in their lower reaches for much of the year. In the drought of 1997 the Yellow—China's second-largest river after the Yangtze—was dry up to 600 kilometers (around 370 miles) inland for 226 days. Although this disruption represented just 11 percent of the total river, it was ruinous for many thousands of families who draw subsistence-farming livelihood from it. Such droughts are not one-off occurrences, and water scarcity is becoming much more systemic.

Between 1850 and 1980, for example, 543 medium- and large-sized Chinese lakes (roughly one-third of estimates of China's total lake count) disappeared due to irrigation projects. Sixty percent of China's 669 cities suffered water shortages in 2005, and groundwater overdraft or overuse (when water removal exceeds water replacement) is more than 25 percent in China and continues to rise. Groundwater overdraft has led to many water tables—the top level of water stored underground—falling more than one meter per year, contributing again to less water availability. Such water depletion rates can be devastating, forcing farmers to switch to crops that do not require much water and eventually leaving the increasingly arid land to lay fallow. Overpumping and the redirection of water sources from regions of relative abundance to those that are drier have further exacerbated China's water stress.

China's water utilization is also making a bad situation worse. Water consumption per unit of GDP (the amount of water used to produce a unit of output—say, a ton of soybeans or a bushel of corn) is higher in China than many other countries—five times the world's average level and eight times the American level, reflecting broad inefficiencies in water use in the farming, industrial, and service sectors.

Are Technology-Based Solutions the Answer?

In the run-up to the 2008 Olympics in China, Beijing's Weather Modification Office used two aircraft, a battery of artillery, and rocket launch sites to shoot silver iodine and dry ice into incoming clouds to create rain. The idea was to ensure that no rain would fall on the main sports arena and neighboring sites during the Olympic competition. Any rain clouds that did manage to get through were shot with chemicals that shrank the droplets. Meanwhile, rain was allowed to fall at other areas that the scientists preferred.

Although the use of such technologies is in early stages, there are clearly extended uses as a tool to irrigate agricultural land.[4] Technology can and does—albeit on a limited basis—help to alleviate demand stresses associated with water. Technologies around water renewability, replacement, and desalination as well as water efficiency tools are all steps in the right direction, and the Chinese are taking a leading role in experimentation. The state-of-the-art Beijiang Power and Desalination Plant (southeast of Beijing), which can distill seawater into freshwater, is one such example. The US$4 billion Beijiang plant is part of a broader effort to establish a national desalination industry over the next five years. More generally, the Chinese government is aiming to supply freshwater to the country and possibly to the world at large. Specifically, this will require that China quadruple its freshwater production from around 180 million gallons (680,000 cubic meters) in 2011 to a staggering 800 million gallons (3 million cubic meters) by 2020.

Scientific and technological innovations—fertilizers, genetically modified crops, mechanized farming irrigation projects—have helped improve crop yields and, hence, contributed to reducing food shortages. However, growth in agricultural yields has, over time, declined. For example, in the 1960s staple crop yields in the West were rising by 3 to 6 percent a year; in recent years they have collapsed to 1 to 2 percent, and the yields across impoverished countries are languishing around flat. It's not just that agriculture yields have to rise in order to cater to global food pressures; in order to have a substantial impact, crop yields have to rise faster than population growth. For now, though, population growth is far outpacing crop yields, and this is a problem.

Given its population pressures and poverty statistics, China faces disproportionate stress in feeding its citizens and making sure they have adequate water supplies. Creating rain is one thing, but even more so China will increasingly need to rely on a range of technology-based solutions (for desalination, irrigation, etc.), particularly when dealing with finite resources and no obvious substitutes, such as arable land and water.

But China cannot do this alone. Other countries (particularly those with more advanced economies) need to prioritize these issues as well. China is, after all, still a low-income country (though number two in the world in GDP terms, it is around number one hundred on per capita income terms). This means China has a long way to go in building the culture, academic expertise, and infrastructure necessary to create the foundation for R&D capable of generating cutting-edge and revolutionary technological solutions.

A Double Whammy

The world is facing an unprecedented catastrophe brought about by a "double whammy"—an increased demand for food and clean water driven by burgeoning populations coupled with the relative scarcity of inputs (arable land, water). For example, although the UK currently produces 60 percent of its own food, a 2009 government report suggested that in just twenty years the average UK diet could resemble that of the Second World War, when there were rations on everything from meat to bread, sugar, tea, cheese, eggs, milk, and cooking fats—all driven by supply impediments. As home to the world's largest population, and given its plans for economic growth, China has its work cut out. And to make matters worse, it is not just the scarcity of land and water that pose a threat to livelihoods to China (and the world over); the rapid depletion and exhaustion of the supply of oil and mineral resources are also cause for alarm. Shortages of nonrenewable resources are exacerbated by hitting their supply upper limits, and supplies that do exist experience rapid depletion. This is not just the domain of land and water but also of energy sources and minerals. To put this in context, it is the landscape of global supply of oil and minerals as well as how China fits into the demand-supply story, to which we now turn.

CHAPTER 3

The Resource State of Play:
Oil, Gas, and Minerals

IN 1956 M. King Hubbert, an American geoscientist, developed a predictive model that accurately forecast that US oil production would peak sometime between 1965 and 1970. His prognosis for the United States, commonly referred to as peak-oil theory, would come to pass when by the early 1970s Hubbert's peak was reached. US oil production was then 10.2 million barrels a day, and it has since been on the decline.

A Peek at Oil

Hubbert's success spawned numerous variants—models formed to forecast the rise and, critically, fall in production of oil fields all around the world. Much as in the US case, the focus has been to predict as closely as possible the point at which the earth's supply of oil will no longer be able to meet the world's energy needs.

While the demand for oil has crept up from twenty million barrels of oil a day in 1960 to around eighty-five million barrels a day (equating to some thirty billion barrels per year) in 2010, oil production has steadily kept pace; increasing from around two billion barrels per annum in the 1930s to thirty billion barrels per annum in 2010. But though global oil supply has largely kept up with demand, we've seen sharp price spikes in response to stresses between supply-demand. For example, the Arab embargo in retaliation for US support for Israel in the October 1973 Yom Kippur War led the

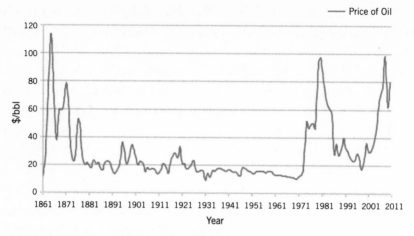

Figure 3.1. Crude oil prices per year, 1866–2011

Source: BP Statistical Review 2006, Platts.

price of petrol to quadruple in just a few months. In the run-up to the 2008 financial crisis the price of a barrel of oil rose to around US$145, multiples higher than the roughly US$20 average over the previous four decades. And again, starting in the winter of 2012, concerns of rising tensions with Iran and rising risks of global oil shortages saw oil breach US$100 a barrel.

Increases in global demand have been an important driver of price rises, as have challenges to global energy supply. Looking ahead, the energy picture will be increasingly destabilized as the gulf between rising global demand and finite supply widens and becomes more precarious, with the global supply picture being of particular consternation.

In 2011 Russia and Saudi Arabia were the top-two oil-producing countries in the world, between them producing roughly 20 million barrels of oil a day of the 85 million barrel daily global demand. Their production, however, is barely enough to cover the oil demand of America alone (roughly 19 million barrels a day). (In practice the United States produces approximately 8.5 million barrels a day and imports the balance—almost 11 million barrels a day).

Beyond the nineteen million barrel US daily demand, if you add in the oil consumption requirements of the next nine countries with voracious appetites for oil (in order in 2010: China, Japan, Russia, India, Germany, Brazil, Saudi Arabia, Canada, and South Korea), you come up with an additional demand of thirty million barrels a day, and the global oil supply-demand picture quickly starts to look very shaky. Today, just over 5 percent of the world's countries consume nearly 60 percent of the world's oil production. This skew adds to global resource pressure by creating a schism between the haves and the have-nots.

Given that this book is about China's global resource campaign, it is imperative that we understand the specific dynamics around its energy supply. However, as in the previous chapter, consideration of China's energy needs and wants must be placed in the broader context of the global supply picture—both today and projected for tomorrow.

A Foreboding Future

The International Energy Agency (IEA)[1] raised the alarm in 2008, projecting a near 50 percent decline in conventional oil production by 2020 and a significant potential gap between supply and demand by 2015.

According to the IEA's World Energy Outlook 2008, in order to meet the world demand forecasts for oil in 2030, "Some 64 million barrels per day of additional gross capacity—the equivalent of almost six times that of Saudi Arabia's production today—need to be brought on stream between 2007 and 2030." Moreover, the IEA suggests that an expenditure of at least US$450 billion per year is needed to sustain oil production and increase overall output to 104 million barrels per day by 2030.

Such oil-demand forecasts place inordinate additional pressure on the world's leading oil producers. The Oil Producing Exporting

Countries (OPEC) will have to increase production by nearly 80 percent by 2030 in order to meet projected oil demand. Yet a report by the UK Energy Research Council notes that worldwide production of conventionally extracted oil could "peak" and go into terminal decline before 2020 and that there is a "significant risk" that global oil production could begin to decline in the next decade.

Predictions from the Peak Models

New peak analysis models offer a brief reprieve—a glimmer of hope that oil stresses will hit later than projected—but the fact that the world already operates near capacity suggests that further reductions in global oil supply will be biting. Because oil-based energy is at the heart of a modern economy (which is powered by turbines, the automotive industry, aviation, computing, etc.), oil price increases inevitably permeate the whole economy: at the pump for commuters as well as across the whole range of transported goods and services, including commodities such as agricultural foodstuffs and minerals that have to be moved from farms and mines to processing plants and refineries and, finally, to neighborhood supermarkets. Oil products also play an important role in agriculture as an input to fertilizers and pesticides, reflecting a cross-dependency between different commodities. Ultimately, of course, higher costs would be borne by higher sticker prices to individuals and households.

But that's only the micro part. At the macro level the countries that produce and export oil (e.g., across the Middle East) would enjoy enormous cash windfalls, improve their trade positions, and make their economies richer. Meanwhile, those countries that rely heavily on energy imports—including the United States and Europe, which imports around 30 percent of gas from Russia—would see their trade positions worsen, as they pay more money to import oil and earn relatively less money from the goods and services they export.

The Supply Crunch

First, the worst news: the major oil fields on earth—whether on land or beneath the sea—have been discovered. In fact, as Figure 3.2 shows, the last major oil discoveries were made between the 1950s and 1960s, and today we are living off the production of these dated discoveries. Not that this has stopped the most optimistic of oil hunters, with the most up-to-date and advanced technologies, from scouring the earth for oil.

Indeed, forecasts out to 2050 indicate that large oil discoveries are tapering off—and tapering off fast. On the current schedule oil discoveries, currently around five billion barrels a year, will progressively decline to around two billion barrels annually by 2050, reverting to discovery and production levels last seen in the 1930s. Already, as depicted on the chart, since the early 1980s total new discovery volumes have steadily and consistently fallen below annual production. If oil production simply lags discoveries, then we can expect that oil supply will soon start rapidly depleting.

To make matters worse, the discovery of new giant (or monster) oil fields, on which world consumption heavily depends, has waned since the 1970s. Today around 1 percent of the world's oil fields, around 500, are classified as giants—and even fewer, only 116, produce more than one hundred thousand barrels a day. In total, these 500-odd oil fields contain more than five hundred million barrels of oil and represent some 60 percent of world supply, with the largest 20 churning out roughly 25 percent of world production.

Looking ahead, overreliance is set to continue. The top ten oil fields of the future (some already under development, although not yet producing oil) are thought to be predominantly located in the Middle East, extending the dominance in energy that the region already has. Consider, for instance, that at current global oil consumption rates (eighty-five million barrels a day, approximately thirty billion barrels a year), the one hundred billion–barrel Iranian field alone could power the world for three years.

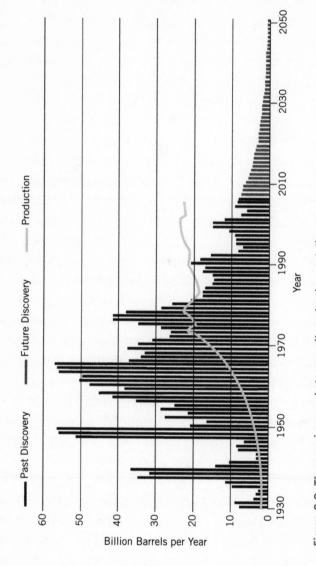

Figure 3.2. The growing gap between oil production and discovery

Source: Colin J. Campbell, *An Atlas of Oil and Gas Depletion* (Huddersfield, West Yorkshire, UK: Jeremy Mills Publishers, 2009).

Table 3.1. The top-ten oil fields of the future

Name	Location	Barrels of recoverable oil (billions)	World oil consumption coverage
Khuzestan	Iran	100	3 years
North Slope	Alaska	40	1.3 years
Ghawar	Saudi Arabia	30	1 year
Khurais	Saudi Arabia	27	10 months
West Qurna	Iraq	21	8 months
Rumaila	Iraq	17	7 months
Carabobo	Venezuela	15	6 months
Majoon	Iraq	13	5 months
Kashagan	Kazakstan	9	3.5 months
Tupi	Brazil	8	3 months

Source: Christopher Helman, "The World's Biggest Oil Reserves," Forbes, January 21, 2010, http://www.forbes.com/2010/01/21/biggest-oil-fields-business-energy-oil-fields.html.

Many of the largest oil fields are over fifty years old. In their aged state their capacity to supply oil declines over time, and post-peak, these declines occur at an accelerating rate. In fact, some of the world's largest oil fields have gone from the highest peak oil production to trough—that is, bottoming out at lower oil production levels in just a few decades.

The Prudhoe Bay oil fields in Alaska, for example, went from nearly 2 million barrels a day production in the mid-1980s to around 500,000 barrels per day in 2000. Over a similar period, the Samotlor oil field in Russia declined from nearly 3 million barrels a day to around 500,000 barrels per day. And the oil field in Slaughter, Texas, saw its production plummet from a peak of nearly 140,000 barrels a day to close to 50,000 barrels a day in 2000. Finally, over a thirty-year period the Romashkino oil field in Russia had its output plunge from over 1.5 million barrels a day peak in 1970 to 500,000 barrels a day in 2000. All this lower oil production points to a worsening global supply picture.

Never mind falling numbers of new discoveries or diminishing oil giants, the implications of broader oil field decay on energy supply is staggering. Schlumberger, an engineering firm, estimates the decline in oil production from existing oil fields out to 2030 to be around 4.3 percent. In particular, if nothing else happens, natural declines from existing fields will see 2010's daily oil supply of approximately 85 million barrels fall to 30 million barrels a day by 2030. Again, this output erosion stems only from natural oil field decay.

The approaching supply picture is troublesome not only because of issues around the depleting stock of oil or the relative overdependence on just a handful of large oil fields; it's also hampered by the mounting costs that make investment in the oil and gas industry restrictive and, ultimately, limit supply.

The oil industry is a colossally expensive undertaking. Exploration, rigs, tankers, floating production, storage and offloading units costs alone can run into the multibillion dollars, meaning the energy business demands enormous amounts of capital. That says nothing of the costs of risks associated with injuries and fatalities that can occur—insurance being part of these costs. Of course, other industries face set-up and operational costs that run sky-high, but getting involved in the energy business (even for relatively small operations) can easily run into the billions of dollars, often with incredibly low odds of success, on the order of one in one hundred tries.

Oil, Freedom, and Corruption

Very often this cost structure means national governments take the lead in the oil sector, placing a country like cash-rich China in prime position to get involved. Government involvement in the resource sector has tended, particularly in emerging economies, to be a source of corrupt activity, and China's escapades in the resource sector have been (unfairly) criticized for tacitly contributing to corruption in resource countries, if not de jure, at least de facto.

The ease with which some government officials tap and divert oil revenues for personal use explains why some of the world's most oil-rich countries are also ranked as the most corrupt. According to the 2011 Transparency International Corruption Perceptions Index, major oil-producing countries such as Nigeria, Indonesia, Angola, and Iraq rank among the most corrupt countries in the world. The evidence simply reflects the fact that much of the so-called rent-seeking (an economics term for corruption or graft) is driven by the rent that is oil.

Beyond the enormous downside risk of corruption lies a more fundamental problem with government involvement in the oil sector. When public finances are stretched and budgets are tight, as they have been across much of the world after the financial crash of 2008, or when competing projects take precedence, the resource industry can suffer from serious underinvestment, whether from the private sector or state-owned actors in the form of national oil companies. As a consequence, oil supply is dramatically reduced over time.

One school of thought held by some economists, traders, and opinion makers argues that we are not running out of oil—that there are as many as three trillion barrels remaining across the earth that could be extracted, whether through better techniques, shale oil and gas finds, or even oil that may become available under shrinking icecaps.

At a practical level this seems wholly unlikely. After all, the rising costs of petrol at the pump and the untold (human) costs of having to resort to warfare to secure energy are simply too high a price to pay if such vast energy sources do exist. But subscribers to this "three trillion barrel" view argue that the structural problem we face is underinvestment in the sector. Underinvestment, they contend, has placed binding constraints on the inputs required to extract the oil, driven costs higher, and led to lower profitability, less investment, and, ultimately, a reduction in oil production and supply.

In support, they point to a crucial fact: that overall oil-producing capacity—which includes tanker usage, refinery usage, and the use of drilling rigs—often hovers around 100 percent—that is, at maximum capacity usage. Tightness in supply markets and capacity has drawn governments into action with some suggestions that between 2011 and 2020 National Oil Companies (NOCs) and government-led companies of the sort China is renowned for will be involved in 90 percent of refining capacity expansion.

Oil production capacity is, of course, regularly hampered by extreme weather swings accompanied by peak demand. During very cold periods when consumers demand greater energy to heat their homes or in hot months when demand for more energy to keep their environments cool (e.g., to run air conditioning units), the infrastructure to deliver greater energy supplies is often pushed to its limits. But more fundamentally, rising average global economic growth at around 5 percent a year and the accompanying effects of energy demand impose serious capacity constraints, particularly when investment lags. Shortages in skilled manpower, such as petroleum engineers to staff the energy business, and the costs of other raw material inputs themselves, such as steel, all feed into higher cost-based inflation, which further discourages investment. Concerns about cost increases in the sector are borne out in the data.

In the four years before the 2008 financial crisis hit in earnest, operating and capital costs in the oil industry doubled, and in the decade between 1999 and 2009 costs rose some 18 percent per annum. Both cost rises are attributed to major underinvestment in the sector over the preceding two decades. The costs to produce oil—from exploration, to extraction, to development—are linked to profitability and, thus, oil supply.[2]

The Price to Make a Profit

For petroleum producers, extraction costs largely determine where the oil price has to be to achieve a profitability of 10 percent. In the OPEC Middle East, where oil production costs are relatively low thanks to the fact that oil is easily accessible and tends to sit in enormous, highly concentrated pools close to the earth's surface, investors can make a 10 percent return with oil trading at just US$20 per barrel. Thanks to oil prices trading as high as US$100 per barrel in recent times—and because the Middle East region accounts for around 40 percent of the world's proven oil and 23 percent of natural gas reserves—countries in the Middle East have accumulated vast wealth. For (other) conventional energy sources, oil needs to trade at around US$25 per barrel in the markets to make a 10 percent return.

Meanwhile, for deepwater oil the 10 percent profit comes only around US$40, whereas for ultradeepwater the trade only works at an average US$60. Extraheavy oil and Arctic oil need to trade at US$80 a barrel in the markets to make the 10 percent, and oil shales, despite their recent popularity, are the most expensive of all, at around US$120 (more on shale later).

More generally, in order to make the oil trade work in most markets, oil needs to trade around US$50 per barrel of oil. At or below US$50 per barrel, many companies are fighting for their survival and can face severe losses or even bankruptcy. For much of the industry oil prices need to be well above US$50 per barrel for a business to be sustainable. Indeed, below US$50 per barrel most non-OPEC projects are uneconomical, leading to project delays, cancellations, difficulties in financing projects, and, ultimately, at the macro level, shortfalls in oil supply. Herein lies the vicious cycle. As it gets more difficult to extract oil from harder-to-reach places, the risks of cost inflation head in only one direction—higher. And this once again limits global supply—at a time when demand is certain to rise.

Petro Politics

The politics of oil complicates the global energy supply picture further.

Most prosperous countries, with the exception of Norway, import oil. Meanwhile, most oil—Norway again excepted—is controlled by powerful, often fabulously wealthy, frequently tyrannical ruling families or closed political cartels. Thus, in one fashion or another much of the industrialized world is beholden to a whole range of despotic, even dangerous oil-supplying nations.

The fact is, though, that governments prefer striking oil deals with tyrannical regimes to looking for alternatives to traditional sources of energy. To preserve the status quo, governments otherwise seemingly deeply committed to freedom in all regards are willing to disregard human rights—or at least not prioritize democratic principles. Such transactions establish an equilibrium that focuses both the seller and the buyer on the short term with almost complete disregard for what such relations imply in the longer term.

Still, the implications for the ideal of liberal democracy should not be ignored. The fact that the world's most influential and economically powerful nations are willing to trade with the most venal and nondemocratic regimes on earth (as long as they have oil) ultimately prevents a free and fair democracy from emerging in these countries, as locals cannot hold their governments accountable for their actions. Furthermore, because the control of resources is pooled (2 percent of the world's population controls 52 percent of oil, 3 percent of the world's population control 54 percent of gas) economies that import these forms of energy are in essence held hostage to the political system and regimes of the countries from which they import.[3]

But there is more. The fact that the oil exporter has a "guaranteed" cash inflow means the oil windfalls replace a government's dependence (broadly speaking) on taxpayers' receipts. Thus, the government cares less about what its domestic constituents want. In essence, the vast oil receipts sever the connection between the individual and government, thereby undermining the veracity and sanctity of the (implicit) democratic contract between them.

No wonder that author and journalist Tom Friedman has described what he calls a first law of petro politics: the correlation between the price of oil and the pace of freedom tend to move in opposite directions. The higher the price of oil (and thus the greater the cash benefit to be earned by the oil seller), the lower the degree of freedom—and vice versa. The ever-present risk in environments where freedoms are lacking is political instability. Saudi Arabia and Russia (the world's leading oil producers) have notoriously tenuous reputations in this regard, but these countries are by no means exceptions.

The counterview to this is that vast oil windfalls can in fact help ensure political stability. The political elite in oil-producing countries, so this argument goes, have greater means and deeper pockets to pay or bribe their citizens, thus keeping them happy and pliant. Under such circumstances, political unrest and contagion is less likely even in the absence of freedoms. Think of Saudi Arabia as an example, where the monarchy is thought to have spent billions on social programs such as education and health to keep opposition and civil unrest at bay—particularly during the 2011 Arab Spring uprisings.

The reality lies somewhere in between. Governmental attitudes are dynamic. At times of relative peace, for instance, governments care less about their domestic citizenry and instead focus on how much money they can get from their foreign buyers and counterparties, whereas in periods of greater domestic disquiet and political volatility, the political establishment looks inward, choosing to transfer cash payments and gifts to the broader population to quell uprisings. Either way, the ultimate interest of the ruling class is largely in the preservation of the status quo, with its unfettered access to oil wealth. It is against this backdrop that China's resource machinations play out.

Location, Location, Location

About four-fifths of the world's known petroleum reserves lie in politically unstable or contested areas. This is why countries such as the United States continue to depend on energy imports from some of the most politically suspect and unstable countries and regions on earth. But where oil is located around the globe also feeds directly into global supply considerations—and China's strategy to secure resources. In essence, the more difficult the political environment of the country or region where oil is located, the more difficult it is to access global oil supplies in a sustained and reliable way. This invariably leads to higher prices and, in the worst case, conflict. This is a trend that is certain to accelerate.

Nigeria offers a case in point. As of September 2010 the United States was importing as much as 15 percent of its crude imports from Nigeria. Add in crude from Angola, Gabon, Equatorial Guinea, and Congo Brazzaville—all politically notorious regimes—and sub-Saharan Africa provides around 20 percent of daily US oil imports.

Dependence on such a coterie of autocratic and often unstable countries has costs beyond simply exposing the inconvenient truth of double standards. Nigeria's ongoing political problems present a perennial disruption risk to physical oil supplies and can drive energy prices higher. The combination of constant power struggles, political jockeying, and sporadic violence around the oil-rich Niger Delta has led to oil shut-ins to the tune of eight hundred thousand to one million barrels per day. Shut-ins occur when outputs fall short of production estimates, or put differently, the oil is available to supply world demand, but it is not being produced (this can be mandated by a company in order to carry out equipment maintenance or due to political instability that makes oil production unsafe). For example, in Nigeria's case, a one million–barrel-a-day shut-in means that Nigeria produces roughly 30 percent less in oil than it can.

Of course, the United States has restricted alternatives, and it doesn't help that China is competing for African oil as well. Africa now provides about one-third of China's oil imports, second only to the Middle East, which provides about 50 percent (with Iran being the main source of imports). In April 2010 China imported around 20 percent of its crude oil from Angola and about 5 percent from Sudan, which was the second-largest African exporter of crude oil to China. China also has become an attractive oil destination for Saudi Arabia—perhaps a small step away from its traditional oil-for-security US-centric strategy. But the Saudis also want to cut production so they can save more for future generations. The bottom line is this: a world with precarious and unpredictable oil supplies points to higher oil prices, as does China's backstop bid—the fact that China will always be in the market as a buyer to satiate its energy demand.

One perhaps cynical view holds that many oil-exporting countries would prefer to depress global oil supplies and (artificially) raise the price of oil, thereby boosting their oil revenues not only to enrich the ruling class but also to meet domestic needs. For example, although oil is cheap to extract in the Middle East, Saudi Arabia needs oil to trade around US$70 to balance its budget, given its plans for heavy spending on education and infrastructure programs.

And it's not just Saudi Arabia that is incentivized this way. Many (poorer) oil-based economies have large proportions of their populations that are under the age of twenty-five (65 percent in Saudi Arabia, 50 percent in Iran, 60 percent across much of sub-Saharan Africa) and/or living in dire indigence (70 percent in Nigeria live below the poverty line). Earning high-priced oil revenues should help these countries tackle youth unemployment, maintain internal stability, and abate national security risks borne of domestic turmoil. Here again, though, rampant corruption in many of these nations enters the picture. In just three years Nigeria's excess crude account—akin to an oil-based sovereign wealth fund—has been steadily depleted, falling from US$20 billion to around US$1 billion in 2010. One doubts bad investments are the sole explanation.

More generally, the OPEC cartel meets regularly to direct oil production and thereby (implicitly) to influence and defend the floor oil price. Of the eighty-five million barrels of oil supplied to the global market each day, almost thirty-five million are attributable to these twelve OPEC members.

Power politics in many other countries around the world also matter to global oil supply. Whether it's Indonesia or Venezuela—both of which have established records of political turmoil—or Iran, whose relations with the West are at a new low, oil and politics are inextricably linked, very often to the detriment of overall global oil production and ultimately the price paid at the pump.

The political intransigence of Iran—the fourth-largest oil producer in the world based on 2010 estimates—regularly casts uncertainty around its four million–barrel-a-day output. Moreover, Iran's reluctance to host UN inspectors and fears around its uranium accumulation and nuclear proliferation program lead to brand-new anxieties about the security of the strategically located Strait of Hormuz—bordered by Iran and the only sea passage to the open ocean for much of the oil-exporting Persian Gulf—and, thus, Gulf energy supplies.

The world has grown accustomed to oil politics, whether spawning domestic conflict or fomenting international clashes where stronger aggressors invade weaker countries to claim dominion over the spoils. The backdrop of rising cost, depleting oil wells, and oil politics makes for depressing reading. It also raises the question of what some of the possible alternatives to oil energy might be.

Hydrocarbons Are Here to Stay

Any basic business text on industry analysis will describe how and why an industry attracts a range of substitutes when it becomes cost heavy and uneconomical. In a world of runaway costs and depreciating assets such as those facing the oil industry, the idea of energy substitutes is no exception, and indeed the chase has been on for some time. China, for example, has become a global leader in wind-technology development.

China has the largest installed capacity of wind energy of any country, around 62,000 megawatts out of a global total of 238,000 megawatts. And a large proportion of all the hot water in Beijing is provided by passive solar water heaters, making China a global leader in solar energy too. Yet the reality is that alternative, renewable energy sources are (a) still in their relative infancy in terms of acceptance and employment and (b) not directly interchangeable with traditional energy sources in many uses. Despite the costs, the path of oil depletion, and even the deleterious consequences to po-

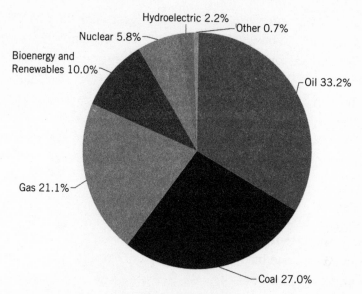

Figure 3.3. Total world primary energy supply by type (percentage)

Source: Benjamin Sporton, World Coal Institute Presentation, Global Coal Dynamics, VI Columbia Minera, October 6, 2010.

litical dynamics and environmental concerns, it's difficult to wean the world off fossil fuels, which means that for the foreseeable future the global economy will remain heavily dependent on hydrocarbons. The chart below shows just how dependent. According to the IEA, the world needs eighty-five million barrels of oil to meet daily global demand. Taken together, hydrocarbons—oil, coal, and natural gas—account for over 80 percent of the total source of global energy. The sources of energy are depicted above.

The chart also introduces us to the second member of the global energy triad, coal, which provides nearly 27 percent of the world's primary energy supply. Roughly 23 million BOE of coal are used worldwide every day. At current rates of production the world's 847 billion tons of coal reserves is enough coal to last us just over a century (around 119 years). By comparison, proven oil and gas reserves are equivalent to only around 46 and 63 years respectively at current production levels. Such statistics have led to some commentators to nickname coal the forgotten fuel.

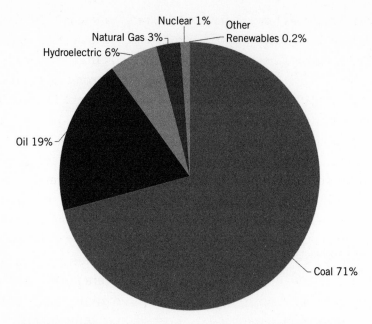

Figure 3.4. Total energy consumption in China by type (percentage)

Source: Milton Catelin, Rock of Ages: The Past, Present and Future of Coal, Chief Executive World Coal Association, Seventh Clean Coal Forum, March 24–25, 2011.

Although coal reserves are thought to be distributed in virtually every country around the world, only around seventy have what are termed recoverable (or proven) reserves—that is, coal resources that are technologically or economically feasible to extract. As in the case of oil, the location of the most important coal deposits worldwide are quite well known, with the biggest reserves lying in the United States, India, and, critically for this discussion, China.

In fact, China's energy consumption is heavily skewed toward coal, as Figure 3.4 shows. China produces and uses about around three billion metric tons annually, making it the largest energy consumption source by a wide margin.[4]

By comparison, the United States consumes roughly one billion metric tons a year, about what China was using fifteen years ago. Given estimates that China has coal reserves that could last a century (US reserves have about two hundred years to go), the concentration of China's coal consumption is unlikely to change soon.

That's the upside of coal. The downside is that continued consumption at such a rate will put China on the wrong side of the environment, history, and, perhaps, the fate of the planet. In 2009 China became the largest greenhouse gas emitter in the world, specifically because of its coal usage, highlighting the fundamental problem with coal as an energy source: its enormous environmental costs.

At the front end, coal mining releases methane from coal seams and the surrounding rock area. In fact, coal mining is thought to be responsible for close to 10 percent of global methane emissions from human activities. At the back end—and the greater danger—burning coal for energy produces waste carbon dioxide that, if not captured and stored, could raise the earth's average global temperatures by more than two degrees. This, environmentalists argue, would take global temperatures above the generally accepted threshold at which it is thought climate change becomes dangerous and possibly irreversible.

Less discussed are the huge volumes of water used in coal-fired power plants. By some estimates, a typical five hundred–megawatt coal-fired power plant uses annually over two billion gallons of water, drawing from nearby sources—lakes, rivers, or oceans—in order to create steam for turning its turbines.

Today coal generates half of the electricity in the United States, more than two-thirds of the electricity in India, and more than three-quarters of the electricity in China. The IEA expects demand for coal to grow by more than two-thirds in the next twenty years, as countries like China and India grow their economies and use their coal deposits.[5]

The Promise of Gas

That gets us to the third member of the energy triad—natural gas. In November 2010 the US Energy Information Administration grabbed headlines with the announcement that domestic proven reserves in natural gas had soared significantly.[6] In particular, the net proven natural gas reserves had risen 11 percent to total 284 trillion cubic feet. This estimate was the highest level since 1971.

The US EIA pronounced these revised estimates (as well as new estimates on US crude oil) as increases that "demonstrate the possibility of an expanding role for domestic natural gas and crude oil in meeting both current and projected US energy demands." Nothing has offered the promise of changing the global energy landscape as much as natural gas. But does this news really signal a turning point or an energy-worry reprieve? There are those who would beg to differ.

Estimates from 2010 suggest that the global production from existing gas fields out to 2030 will decline by around 5.35 percent per year. Furthermore, natural decay from existing fields will see the global supply of approximately 55 million BOE natural gas per day produced in 2010 fall to 20 million BOE a day by 2030. In a Supply Gap Analysis, Schlumberger finds that demand for oil and gas is projected to grow at 1 percent and 1.8 percent respectively over the period, taking us to total daily demand estimates of close to 180 million barrels a day and a shortfall of at least 30 million barrels of oil a day by 2030.[7]

Yet another harbinger of the impending energy stresses and shortfalls.

The Challenge of Interchanging

The supply trajectory of the main plausible substitutes for oil does not provide much comfort, and even if it did, the fact is that most energy sources are not perfect substitutes for each other.

Whereas oil has broadly three uses—70 percent transportation (vehicles, planes, trains, vessels), 20 percent chemical (e.g., petrochemicals), and 10 percent other (boiler fuel, asphalt, electrical feedstock), natural gas has basically two uses: as a heat source (direct heat, feedstock for power generation) and chemical feedstock (feedstock is the raw material for the production of a compound substance).[8] Coal, for its part, provides electricity and is an essential fuel for steel and cement production as well as other industrial activities.

If weaning the world off fossil fuels is not an immediate option, and if the production path of energy sources is precarious with substantive costs—and if, in fact, energy sources are not perfectly substitutable—what choices do we have? Improvements in energy efficiency are one way to garner improvements, but the trend in the last decade has been disappointing.

Although energy efficiency improved by about 2 percent per annum in the 1970s and 1980s, this trend fell to 1 percent per annum in the 1990s. The risk is this: if no further technology advancements are made, then energy demand in 2030 will be approximately 35 percent higher than it will be if technology keeps improving the energy efficiency at the same rate it has over recent years.

Technology as a Saving Grace

In January 2011 media outlets issued reports of Brazilian oil deposits that would boost Brazil's reserves to an astounding 123 billion barrels—equivalent to roughly four years of oil supplies at current world consumption rates.

Amid the euphoria of the megafind, one could have been excused for overlooking the major caveat on this seemingly good news: Brazil's oil deposits in the Atlantic Ocean lay below a layer of salt two miles below the ocean surface and another two to four miles beneath the seabed. Even conservative estimates suggest that access to the oil treasure would cost billions of dollars. The Brazilian oil giant, Petrobras, which had sixteen billion barrels of proven reserves at the time of this writing, had plans to invest more than US$200 billion in five years. Yet even with unlimited amounts of cash, burrowing through the salt layer would require significant advances in technology. Indeed, according to oil experts, the existence of the Brazilian oil find has always been known; it's only now through technological advancements that there is a *chance* to gain access to it—albeit at substantial cost.

Technology has helped and continues to help address the supply-and-demand imbalance in the oil sector. If limiting demand is not an option—which for all intents and purposes it is not unless, of course, punitive taxes on oil consumption are imposed—then technology will have to step forward via advanced exploration strategies or even in creating or finding energy substitutes.

It's not an impossibility. New innovations in technology led to many of the discoveries in the 1950s and 1960s, and technology ensured that world reserves would increase over the last twenty years—both for oil and gas. According to the BP Statistical Review, the increase of historical oil and gas reserves can nearly wholesale be attributed to technology-related increases in reserves driven by improved recovery factors (the amount of energy that can be extracted from a particular basin) in known reservoirs. The worldwide average recovery factor is up to around 32 percent, from approximately 20 percent in previous decades.

McKinsey, the global consulting firm, argues that a US$170 billion a year program that targets cost-effective ways to increase energy productivity could halve the growth in energy demand and cut emissions of greenhouse gas. Rising energy demand and higher commodity prices attract greater investment to the sector and could help to stimulate the development of new technologies, materials, and processes that enable resource firms to search for new deposits and bring within reach those deposits that were once considered inaccessible.

Technological breakthroughs in US gas production have meaningfully improved the economics of unconventional gas opportunities. In fact, there exists a real risk that such rapid improvements in technology development of global gas reserves and liquefaction capacity have created a global glut of natural gas. It is too early to tell what the overall impact of gas finds will be, but whatever it proves to be, technology is not a panacea for all energy ills.

For example, although new extraction techniques can yield additional sources of natural gas, the energy returned on energy invested will be much lower than traditional gas sources, and this inevitably leads to higher costs to natural gas consumers. Furthermore, technology cannot completely reverse demographic and environmental pressures; some countries and regions will simply be unable to afford the higher costs of alternative technologies. Beyond this, new and promising alternative techniques to source energy, such as hydraulic fracturing (fracking), face environmental resistance, signaling that their benefits are far from a foregone conclusion.

Because oil is not a renewable energy source, it will be exhausted at some point in the future and, thus, should not be depended on as a long-term solution. However, without convincing efficiency improvements, revolutionary strides in technology, and the discovery of credible alternative energy sources, traditional energy sources are the only source the world will continue to turn to in order to meet energy demand through 2030—the upcoming two decades when China is going to be most radically accelerating its energy consumption.

Convergence on the Cards

To place China's specific energy needs in context, let's compare the two largest economies in the world by GDP. China is home to approximately 1.3 billion people—around 20 percent of the global population. With roughly 310 million people, the United States represents less than 5 percent of the world's current population of nearly 7 billion. Yet the US population guzzles 25 percent of today's global oil consumption while also contributing roughly 20 percent to world GDP. This translates to America consuming around 20 million barrels a day, or 25 barrels per person per year. Meanwhile China consumes just 9 percent of the world's oil, translating to total daily consumption approaching 9 million barrels a day, or 2.2 barrels per person per year. (As a quick side comparison, India's 1.1

billion people consume 3 million barrels a day, or a barrel per person per year.)

But what happens as China (and, of course, other emerging countries) converges to higher levels of oil consumption? Are there enough energy resources so a billion Chinese can live like three hundred million Americans? Take transportation, for example, which accounts for more than 50 percent of oil consumption. Imagine the implications for oil demand as China—with thirty-five cars per thousand people—converges to US levels of roughly 800 cars per thousand people.[9]

Already, between 2000 and 2009 growth in oil consumption went up 50 percent in China, 30 percent in the Middle East, 12 percent in India, 11 percent in South America, and 8 percent across Africa. (Other parts of Asia posted around 1 percent growth.) The International Energy Agency predicts that world oil demand is set to rise by 45 percent by 2030, from around 85 million barrels a day to close to almost 120 million barrels of oil a day. There are no signs of this abating. Land, water, and energy supplies (in the form of oil and gas) are already feeling the squeeze of demand pressures arising from demographic changes across the globe. So too are metals and mineral deposits around the world, as we discuss next.

Upwardly Mobile

China's impressive economic record has had a marked impact on domestic incomes, and incomes have a dramatic effect on the consumption of all sorts of goods and services. As we've discussed, metals and minerals such as copper, cobalt, platinum, and iron are all inputs for vehicles, mobile phones, and the construction of buildings, so as demand for these finished products has risen over time, so too has demand for metals and minerals.

According to the investment bank UBS, US$13,000 is the per capita income level at which a population's consumption increases dramatically. Already urban China boasts some fourteen million

Chinese whose incomes average US$10,000 per year, and the per capita GDP in cities like Shanghai matches income levels in South Korea in 1997, when consumption there of all manner of goods and services skyrocketed.

Consumption measures the aggregate value of goods and services bought by a population and is often the largest component of GDP. Yet while China is now the second-largest economy in GDP terms, it ranks only fifth in consumption: 35 percent of its GDP goes to consumption, compared to 70 percent in the United States, around 60 percent across Europe, and roughly 50 percent in India. Not one to leave anything to chance, the Chinese government has turned its focus to this vexing issue, aiming to increase consumption to around 50 percent of GDP over the next several decades.

Indeed, increasing consumption spending was a central aspect of China's Twelfth Five-Year Plan for National Economic and Social Development, issued in October 2010. This five-year plan lays out a broad range of policies to help boost Chinese consumption, all of which bode well for demand of metals and minerals that are used in construction, telecommunications, the automotive industry, shipping, and, of course, the full complement of "white goods" (refrigerators, stoves, washing machines, air conditioners, etc.). More specifically, if China's plans materialize and urbanization gets to 75 percent in 2050 (from 45 percent in 2010), increases in consumption and, thus, the knock-on effects on minerals would be enormous.

However, not all minerals are equal. Some have a lot of relevance to China's great ascendancy, whereas others have less. Two questions help narrow down the "relevant to China" criteria. First, does the mineral feed into China's urbanization story—as a critical input for construction and so forth, as listed earlier? Second, is China structurally short of the mineral? That is, do China's demands (grossly) outweigh its supply (China's production plus its imports)? Based on these two tests, only one mineral satisfies both criteria: copper.[10]

Copper is used in wires and cables and electrical transmission. More generally, it is used for plumbing and heating systems, air conditioners, washing machines, refrigeration, telecommunication cables, power cables, semiconductors, motors for heavy appliances, equipment and machinery, industrial valves and fittings; copper pervades many aspects of modern-day living.

In 2006 China's share of global consumption of refined copper was 23 percent, less than that of the Organization for Economic Co-operation and Development (OECD) economies at 54 percent but equal to copper demand of all other major emerging markets.[11] By the end of 2010—that is, in just over five years—China's share of global consumption of refined copper shot up to 41 percent while declining to 35 percent in the OECD and remaining virtually constant across other emerging countries. Of course China can supplement its domestic copper production with imports, but as we discuss later, directly investing in mines around the world increases the certainty of its copper supply that China so desperately needs. Whatever the case, with China's size and appetite, this ascendant curve inevitably stresses supply, and there the picture grows more problematic.

The Challenges of Supply

The prospects for medium- to long-term copper supply are worrisome, and much of the world is ill prepared for the eventualities of such shortfalls.

Much like the oil story described earlier, the world continues to rely on copper deposits from discoveries of days gone by while having to spend more and more money to extract it. Copper is still sourced from world-class deposits such as the El Teniente in Chile, whose discovery dates back to 1910. In theory, there should be nothing wrong with drawing on assets that keep giving, but miners have to go to ever-greater depths to get at the copper. For example, in 1980 all new discoveries with over four million tons of copper were exposed—and, thus, made easier to access. Between 2000 and 2010, however, around 80 percent of new finds were "blind"—discovered by testing far beneath the earth's surface, where the mineral is

Table 3.2. Sourcing copper globally (percentage)

Region's risk level	2000	2020 (est.)
Low risk	62	44
Medium risk	36	47
High risk	2	10

Source: Brook Hunt, a Wood Mackenzie Company, "Metals Market Service—Monthly Update: Copper September 2010," "Metals Market Service—Long Term Outlook, Copper September 2010."

much harder to access. Meanwhile, copper quality has also been declining. In 1980 "head grade treated copper" (the percent of copper found in a metric ton of mined mineral) stood at roughly 1.5 percent. Forecasters expect copper grades to fall to around 1 percent over the next decade—that is, into 2020. Products made of less-pure copper tend to perform less well.

Increasingly, mining companies will have to go farther afield to more risky locations to source copper. As Table 3.3 shows, in 2000 62 percent of copper was estimated to come from low-risk locations, 36 percent from medium-risk places, and only 2 percent from high-risk sites. Fast-forward to 2020, and the expectation is that almost 10 percent of copper will come from regions deemed to be high-risk locations (versus 44 percent in low and 47 percent in medium, respectively).

Meanwhile, mines that are up and running are increasingly beset by operational problems stemming from years of underinvestment in the sector due to low prices during much of the 1980s, 1990s, and early 2000s. The 2010 Copiapó mining accident in Chile is thought by many in the mining industry to have been the consequence of underinvestment, with many components of the mining equipment deemed faulty or too aged for use. Against this backdrop, it comes as no surprise that copper supply almost consistently, year after year, continues to fall short of expectations. This has certainly been true over much of the last decade.

As with other minerals, copper also is prey to the ever-present risk of time-inconsistent policymaking, which hurts global supply.

Time inconsistency is the idea that over time governments choose not to honor or implement policies that were previously agreed on. Time inconsistency in the mining sector—and, indeed, across contracts entered into across the broader commodity complex—is both pervasive and punitive. The saga around the mining tax hike in Australia in 2010, which took many mining companies by surprise, is just one recent example of inconsistency around government policy. Seeking to earn more revenues from the mining sector, the government at first imposed a 40 percent tax on coal and iron-ore mining, later reduced to 30 percent in the face of objections from mining companies. The size of the tax matters less than the fact that it was sprung on the mining industry with little warning, making cost projections almost impossible to hold to, but Australia is hardly alone in changing the rules virtually overnight. Across the world governments—usually motivated by public-sector budget problems—are tearing up and rewriting the laws governing their mining sectors.

China's Consumption versus the World's Production

According to a September 2010 report by the commodity research company Brook Hunt, global copper mine production will decline by 1.2 percent per year between 2010 and 2025, with output falling from a peak of 18.8 metric tons in 2013 to 13.3 metric tons in 2025. This is the base case scenario; it does not take into consideration serious mine disruptions of the type discussed earlier. Over the same period demand for additional mine production will create an implied shortfall in mine output (including the disruption allowance) of around 0.5 metric tons per annum in 2011, worsening to around 13.8 metric tons per annum by 2025.

Meanwhile, China's demand for copper is expected to grow by 6 percent per year between 2009 and 2025, from around 6.5 metric tons at the end of 2009 to about 16.5 metric tons by 2025. This approximate 10-metric-ton gain in China's refined consumption will result in its share of global refined copper consumption increasing from 38 percent at the end of 2009 to a significant 55 percent by 2025. That's the demand picture. The supply picture is where the real issues lie.

China contains roughly 6 percent of the world's copper reserves, but this does little to quell its voracious appetite. For example, whereas the constant annual growth rate (CAGR) for global copper cathode is expected to fall by 0.6 percent between 1980 and 2020 across OECD countries and rise by just 2.7 percent across other countries, it's expected to be up by 9.1 percent in China. If Chinese incomes continue to converge to US levels, that figure will swell accordingly, with no obvious offsetting increase in copper supply. Like the energy story detailed earlier, the precarious global copper supply picture is worsened by the locations of the largest copper deposits. Among the world's top-twenty copper producers are politically unstable countries and economies that lack full market transparency, including Indonesia, Russia, Kazakhstan, Democratic Republic of Congo, and Iran. Such countries account for more than 25 percent of global copper supply, and thus, with its copper production at around 1.1 metric tons—falling far short of its 6.5 metric ton demand—China has little choice but to rely on these countries for copper supply.

Relieving Demand Pressures and Easing Supply Shortfalls

If nothing is done, global copper demand rises versus supply constraints will, over the next several decades, get much worse. But more than just copper; barring a technological revolution of substantial scale, the world is arguably facing seemingly insurmountable constraints across the whole gamut of commodities—arable land, water, energy, and other minerals. Moreover, with China's aggressive rush for resources, many countries are likely to be caught short as the commodity shortages become much more acute and the commodity constraints more severely binding. Save China, which has faced the prospect of the forthcoming global resource disaster and is doing what it can to avert the crisis, the world is ill prepared for a commodity calamity.

The last couple of chapters have presented a snapshot of the rising threat of resource supply shortages—in arable land, water, energy, and minerals. In the chapters that follow we analyze what China is doing in the commodity space, how it is doing it, and the implications for the global commodity markets and geopolitics at large.

CHAPTER 4

Hocking the Family Jewels

THE *New York Times* headline of June 13, 2010, was an eye stopper: "U.S. Identifies Vast Riches of Minerals in Afghanistan." The find—which included huge veins of iron, copper, cobalt, gold, and critical industrial metals like lithium—revealed a treasure trove worth at least US$1 trillion.

As with oil, exploiting such vast mineral riches takes a lot of money. Extraction processes require capital investment in areas largely devoid of the infrastructure necessary for resource extraction. In that regard, China's financial muscle gives it a definite edge, granting access to commodities that other countries can't afford to explore. It is not surprising, then, that by the time the news of the US mineral discovery hit the front page, China had already struck resource deals with the Afghanis, including the Aynak copper mine in Logar Province, at least a year prior.

China's commodity crusade is multifaceted. It encompasses *what* China does to secure the assets, *how* China gains ownership or access to global commodities (using an intricate web of strategies), and what the sheer scope of China's resource rush means for the world. China's resource campaign does not stop at Afghanistan; it's global and seemingly never ending.

Means, Motive, Opportunity—What China Does

China's foray into international resource markets involves a comprehensive three-pronged approach: via financial transfers (be it aid or commercial loans), through trade, and by means of investment.

In regard to financial transfers, whether it is lending to the US government by buying US government bonds, making aid transfers to African countries, or lending money to South American countries, China extracts favors and is able to transact across the globe. The aid strategy has been largely reserved for the poorest countries, and thus mainly targeted at Africa. But although this aid has involved direct cash transfers, as we shall see, even in Africa China's resource approach has gone well beyond simply writing checks. In 2002 China gave US$1.8 billion in development aid to African countries, including pledges to train fifteen thousand African professionals, build thirty hospitals and one hundred rural schools, and increase the number of Chinese government scholarships to African students. Two years earlier, in 2000, China had written off US$1.2 billion in African debt. In 2003 it forgave another US$750 million.

Other countries and regions have been benefiting from China's largesse too, including the United States. In 2011, for example, China was the largest single holder of US government debt, with 26 percent of all foreign-held US Treasury securities (around 8 percent of total US public debt). In 2009 China made a US$50 billion loan to the International Monetary Fund. In the same year, as a way to provide seed money to its trading partners, the People's Bank of China signed a total of 650 billion renminbi (US$95 billion) in bilateral agreements with six central banks: South Korea, Hong Kong, Malaysia, Indonesia, Belarus, and Argentina, sealing China's status as an integral player in these markets. China's approach of lending money and making friends fits snugly into its broader strategy of making deals across the resource space.

Then there is trade.

Trade has been a centerpiece of China's "going-out" strategy, but to some of China's trading partners it has been a bone of contention. The United States has blamed China for a large proportion of American trade deficits over the last several years. Nevertheless, China's ascension as one of the world's foremost exporters has helped improve the livelihoods of tens of millions of people at home by providing employment to vast swaths of the undereducated. And, of course, many consumers around the world (but particularly in the United States) have gained enormously from access to manufactured goods at China's knockdown prices, albeit at the cost of their own domestic manufacturing markets. In 2007 China overtook Canada to become biggest goods importer to the United States. In 2011 the value of US imports (goods) from China was US$399.3 billion, up from US$296.4 billion in 2009.

Meanwhile, in the middle of 2010 China became the largest trading partner of both Brazil and Chile—among the most important economies on that continent. China has become Africa's single-largest trading partner, unseating the United States, which did US$86 billion in trade with Africa in 2009. According to Chris Alden, author of *China in Africa*, two-way trade between China and Africa grew from US$10 billion in 2000, to US$55 billion in 2006, to US$90 billion in 2009.

China's rise as a leading trading trade partner has not been without criticism. In addition to China's controversial exchange rate regime—artificially set to make Chinese exports globally competitive[1]—China has lent increasingly greater amounts of money to its target consumer markets to finance the purchase of Chinese products. For example, in 1995 the US Export-Import Bank issued around US$20 billion of credit lines to countries around the world, for much the same purpose. At that time China had one export credit bank that made US$4 billion in loans. Today, the United States still gives around US$20 billion in credit lines, but China now has five export-import credit institutions that issued almost US$250 billion in loans in 2009—a sixty-fold increase in fifteen years. Such export credit agencies help finance the sales of exports (in this case Chinese exports) to other countries by providing loan guarantees, export-credit insurance, and direct loans. Of course the US-China debt for trade linkages also has the hallmarks of this relationship. Fair or not, this is a trade strategy that has demonstrably worked.

Finally, there is investment.

China's aid and trade strategies alone would make it a powerful international presence, but the nation's investment strategy—and the way it intertwines with and supports the other two elements—puts the Asian upstart in a class of its own.

The fact is that Chinese investment in the resource markets has been transformational for the international landscape, not least because its investment into both hard and soft commodities has been substantial. China's surfeit of capital means that it is capable of funding inputs, infrastructure, and logistics (equipment and transportation), thus exploiting natural endowments and granting the nation access to commodities that are not available to countries that don't have its war chest.

The US-based Heritage Foundation has developed the China Global Investment Tracker, calling it the "only publicly available, comprehensive data set of large worldwide Chinese investments and contracts beyond US Treasury bonds." (Of course, the Chinese government also provides statistics on its outward investment, but that data is not always pooled or easy to decipher.[2]) The tracker provides details of over 250 attempted Chinese transactions—failed and successful—valued at more than US$100 million, in major industries from energy and mining to transportation and banking, starting in 2005.

China Inc. came of age in foreign investing in 2005 when the Chinese corporation Lenovo purchased IBM's PC unit. This was a seminal transaction not only because of the absolute size of the deal (US$1.25 billion) or the iconic status of the seller, but also because the value of this one transaction was more than half the total value of all the international deals China had previously embarked on up to 2005. China's total investment up to and including 2004 had amounted to US$2 billion. Moreover, the Lenovo transaction was part of US$12 billion of Chinese investments in 2005—a defining year in Chinese outward investment and one that lent the nation the confidence and stature to embark on its new "going out" investment strategy.

Spanning the Globe

The Heritage Foundation's database tells us that the Chinese investment campaign has been both enormous—totaling nearly US$400 billion over five years—and global. Between 2005 and 2012 Australia attracted the largest amount (US$42.5 billion) of nonbond investment from China; the United States was second at US$28 billion. Over the same period countries in the Western Hemisphere received a lion's share of China's investment—totaling around US$88 billion—more than the investment that was directed to China's "traditional" partners in East Asia. Virtually every other region—North America, Africa, Europe, East Asia, West Asia (Iran, Kazakhstan, and the Russian Federation), and the Arab world attracted about US$50 billion each.

On a more granular level, data from China's Ministry of Commerce, 2007 Statistical Bulletin of China's Outward Foreign Direct Investment, indicates that the top African recipients of China's outward FDI (South Africa, Nigeria, Sudan, Zambia, Algeria, Niger, Egypt, Mauritius, Ethiopia, DRC, and Angola) took in around US$4 billion—just 4 percent of the world total. In 2006 the bulk of Sino-Africa FDI flows involved the mining sector (40.74 percent), business services (21.58 percent), finance (16.4 percent), transport and telecommunications (6.57 percent), wholesale and retail trade (6.57 percent), and manufactured goods (4.33 percent), with agriculture, forestry, and fisheries attracting less than 1 percent of Chinese FDI.

In 2010 China, already Brazil's largest trading partner, surpassed the US to become Brazil's largest investor. This was a feat achieved in just six months—in 2009 China had ranked only twenty-ninth globally for investment in Brazil. In the first six months of 2010 China increased its investment in Brazil tenfold, to US$20 billion. China plans to build steel factories and auto plants as well as invest in telecommunications infrastructure and agriculture (planting soybean across forty thousand hectares), and China will also help Brazil explore and extract the country's rich offshore oil resources. Indeed, China has committed US$250 billion to the latter goal.

In addition to investment, the China Development Bank will lend US$10 billion to Brazil's state-owned oil company, Petrobras, to help secure its oil supply. As Brazil's new largest trading partner, China also saw its exports to Brazil surge a staggering 57.7 percent year on year to US$10.76 billion in the first six months of 2010, while Brazilian imports to China grew 17.9 percent per year on year to US$13.47 billion over the same period. Thus, trade, aid, and investment all interlock—in Brazil, Africa, and elsewhere.

Vertical and Horizontal Alignment

In 2008 the Chinese struck a deal with the Greek government to manage two piers and container terminals in the Greek port of Piraeus—the main port of Greece, the largest port in Europe, and the third-largest port in the world. For Euro 4.3 billion (roughly US$5.6 billion), Cosco Pacific, China's state-owned shipping company, pledged to increase the capacity of the port by up to 250 percent over thirty-five years.

As this deal suggests, and detailed earlier, China's strategy is not solely to get a full range of commodities from a variety of countries; it also is actively pursuing the underlying infrastructure to ensure that once the resources are extracted, they can be transported back to China in the quickest and most reliable way. To do this, China is investing in ports and buying the shipping assets and transportation links to ferry the resources home.

In fact, China increasingly sets the tone in global shipping and the international seaborne trade. In 2011 Shanghai became the world's largest container port, usurping Singapore. Already, more than half of the world's top-ten container ports are Chinese, and over the next decade it is possible that several other Chinese ports such as Ningbo, Shenzhen, and Guangzhou could also overtake Singapore. Ships go to where the demand flows, as evidenced across global shipping's three major segments: container shipping, dry bulk shipping, and tanker shipping.

Container shipping, used in the transportation of finished goods, continues to be a great indicator of Chinese exports being sent abroad and a very reliable gauge of the strength of the Chinese economy. (In the run-up to the 2007–2008 financial crisis, container shipping was growing in double digits.) As the world's largest producer of crude steel and the largest importer of iron ore, China is central to the dry bulk–shipping business, which is used to transport these as well as other major commodities, like coal. And finally, as the world's second-largest importer of energy, China's importance in tanker shipping—used in the transportation of crude oil and refined products by sea—is key.

China's fleet has also mirrored its growing importance in shipping, increasing from 1,367 to 3,127 vessels in the decade between 2001 and 2011. Today, around 50 percent of China's fleet is built in China by state-owned Chinese companies like Cosco. Of China's fleet, bulk carriers represent the majority of its commercial sea craft, reflecting its voracious appetite for commodities.

China is not the only country adopting this more integrated strategy. In 2010 the Brazilian mining giant, Companhia Vale do Rio Doce (Vale), decided to use its own fleet of four hundred thousand–ton iron ore carriers to transport ore from Brazil to China. (As part of the plan, Vale also pledged to take delivery of the first of thirty-six very large new ore carriers in summer 2011.) Ian Shirreff, the CEO of Shanghai-based Zodiac, which has contracts to bring iron ore to twenty of China's biggest state steel mills, noted that the sheer size and numbers of the ships will drive shipping rates downward over the next decade, probably to the US$10,000 to US$12,000 a day time charter rate seen in 1977. Falling transportation rates mean that China's more integrated approach of securing global resources and then moving the commodities using its own infrastructure is much more cost competitive and also secure.

China's commodity crusade has led it to invest in ports and pipelines in Pakistan, Myanmar, and Sri Lanka as well as in roads and railways in Ethiopia, Argentina, and Ukraine. Whether China is negotiating transport routes with Colombia to rival the Panama

Canal (China-Colombian trade has increased from US$10 million in 1980 to more than US$5 billion in 2010, serving as an impetus) or angling for access to US ports (China Ocean Shipping Corporation's attempt to lease the Long Beach port in 1999 was blocked by US congressional action), one thing is clear: China's resource strategy is not just about using shipping lanes and leading trade routes; it's also about owning the underpinning infrastructure.

How China Does It: The Many Ways to Skin a Cat

Analyzing how China is executing its resource campaign is unwieldy. Matching the array of Chinese buyers (e.g., the Chinese government, individuals, and corporations) with the range of sellers (governments, corporations, individuals across different countries), thus using multiple ways to transact, spews a seemingly infinite number of permutations. But if we focus only on how resource deals are done, then three ways stand out.

First are direct purchases, in which some part of China Inc. takes ownership of an underlying asset, such as land or a mine. The purchase of the mineral rights to Mount Toromocho in Peru, cited at the beginning of this book, is one such example.

Second are swap transactions, in which China locks in the asset off-take—purchasing all production from the asset but never actually buying or taking ownership of the underlying asset. Two examples: in February 2009 China agreed to lend Russian oil companies US$25 billion in return for oil supplies for twenty years. The two countries are also considering building a twenty-five hundred–mile pipeline from Russia's Far East Amur region to Daqing in northeastern China. In a similar vein, in May 2009, alongside a deal to increase Brazil's export of chicken and beef to China, China lent around US$10 billion to Petrobras, Brazil's government-controlled oil company, in exchange for providing two hundred thousand barrels of oil a day to Sinopec (China's state-owned company) for the subsequent ten years.

Table 4.1. China's loans for oil and gas since January 2009

Country	Date	Borrower	What the host country got
Angola	March 13, 2009	Angola government	US$1 billion
Bolivia	April 2009	Bolivian government	US$2 billion
Brazil	Feb. 18, 2009	Petrobras	US$10 billion
Brazil	April 15, 2010	Petrobras	n.a.
Ecuador	July 2009	PetroEcuador	US$1 billion
Ghana	June 2010	GNPC	n.a.
Kazakhstan	April 17, 2009	KMG	US$10 billion
Russia	Feb. 17, 2009	Rosneft	US$15 billion
Russia	Feb. 17, 2009	Transneft	US$10 billion
Turkmenistan	June 2009	Turkmengaz	US$4 billion
Venezuela	Feb. 21, 2009	Bandes (PDVSA)	US$4 billion
Venezuela	Feb. 21, 2009	Bandes (PDVSA) and government	US$10 billion and RMB 70 billion

Source: IEA, 2011.

In a 2011 report, "Overseas Investments by Chinese National Oil Companies," the IEA provides a list of twelve such swap transactions between January 2009 and April 2010. These "loans for long-term oil and gas supply," which totaled US$77 billion over just fifteen months, showcase China's amazing breadth in purpose. For the most part the loans target infrastructure and the build-out of pipelines, roads, ports, and railways as well as agriculture projects. But the interesting point is that although much of the developed world was busy dealing with the aftermath of the 2008 financial crisis, China continued, undeterred.

The third "how" method is indirect access to resources through the international capital markets. An example of this is buying stakes in different corporations, which grants the majority shareholder both the rights to dictate a company's strategy and ownership rights of the asset. Chinese entities gain indirect access to resources by investing in international hedge funds, private equity funds, and other money managers, sometimes for pure financial return but also sometimes to gain equity stakes in commodity companies.

The Chinese strategies of resource investing have become so pervasive that some now have nicknames. Financial market participants often make the distinction between the "Angola mode," which refers to government-to-government infrastructure for resource deals, and the "Addax mode," which refers to buying shares in listed companies, which can then lead to full acquisition of resource companies. The November 2011 agreement by China's state-owned oil company Sinopec to buy a 30 percent stake in the Brazilian unit of Portuguese oil company Galp Energia for US$3.54 billion is an example of the latter. The Sinopec-Galp deal would provide Sinopec with over twenty-one thousand BOE a day in 2015.

What's in It for Me?

In November 2006 more than forty African leaders gathered in Beijing at the first Sino-African summit—the Forum on China-Africa Cooperation. Nearly every sub-Saharan African leader was in attendance, and almost all African countries were represented. The Chinese spared no expense to create the right ambience. The streets were lined with African flags as part of the revelry to make the African delegates "feel more at home." Against this backdrop, the Chinese government unveiled its Africa strategy.

In his opening ceremony address President Hu Jintao told his audience, "In all these years, China has firmly supported Africa in winning liberation and pursuing development. . . . China has trained technical personnel and other professionals in various fields for Africa. It has built the Tanzam Railway and other infrastructure projects and sent medical teams and peacekeepers to Africa." Now, China would strengthen its Pax Sino-Africana ties still further, in the form of new trade initiatives, agricultural cooperation, debt relief, improved cultural ties, health care, training, and some aid.

The motivations for China's resource campaign around the globe are obviously economic and fall directly into the Chinese leadership's articulated policies of poverty alleviation and economic growth. China needs food and fuel as fast as possible and in as vast quantities as possible to guarantee that its future economic performance mirrors that of its recent past.

For China, the most pressing matter at hand is how best to move some eight hundred million people from abject poverty to a modern lifestyle, marked by the trappings of a middle-class existence: washing machines, refrigerators, cars, and the like. With a relatively high income inequality and a dangerous and growing split between the haves and the have-nots, the Chinese government has its work cut out for it. Resources on a large scale are a significant part of remedying the situation. It's a race from a revolution.

But as in Africa and around the world, China is executing its resource strategy with considerable aplomb, doing seemingly everything it can to make certain that commodity deals benefit both signatories to the trades. In fact, the motivation for the host countries is also not complicated: They need infrastructure, and they need to finance projects that can unlock economic growth. To achieve this, they are willing to sell their assets to the highest bidder. This is the genius of the China strategy: every country gets what it wants.

China, of course, gains access to commodities, but host countries get the loans to finance infrastructure developmental programs in their economies, they get to trade (creating incomes for their domestic citizenry), and they get investments that can support much-needed job creation. In 2010 alone, China pledged to lay down US$12 billion in railway lines in Argentina. According to Chris Alden, Chinese foreign direct investment (FDI) flows into Africa were US$48 billion in 2006 and as much as US$88 billion just two years later—much of it earmarked for infrastructure outlays. The raw numbers are important to the host countries, clearly, but so are the secondary benefits. With harrowing statistics like those in the August 2010 International Labour Organisation report, which disclosed that around eighty-one million youth aged between eighteen and twenty-five years old are unemployed, investment and job creation are going to be central to the world's future progress. This is particularly true in countries across the emerging world—in Africa and the Middle East—where upward of 60 percent of the populations are under the age of twenty-four.

Poor countries (and rich countries too) need jobs to stem the risk of social despondency that could escalate the risk of political unrest and insurgency. By building factories and rolling out infrastructure projects and opening mines, China is helping to create those jobs in countries with resources to sell. China has also won friends and plaudits for its efforts in building health care centers and schools. Across the world the most impoverished countries—those that lack both adequate medical and educational facilities and the cash to invest in them—are only too happy to accept China's largesse. These monies help the host governments roll out hospitals and schools that help meet demand in a meaningful way. In countries across Africa, where the incidence and prevalence of disease burdens and literacy rates have significant room for improvement, China's generosity is often preferred to the hectoring that tends to accompany financial support from traditional (Western) aid donors. The 2005 decision by the Bush administration to cut aid funding for condoms across Africa in preference for programs espousing and promoting abstinence is only a dramatic example of a continuing trend that, to many Africans, smacks of hypocrisy and paternalism.

In 2010 an estimated twenty-three million people were living with HIV/AIDS in Africa (around two-thirds of the global total), and literacy rates registered as low as 30 percent (vis-à-vis developed economies where literacy rates are closer to 99 percent). For these countries China's resource-for-infrastructure, -schools, or -health care proposition seems the obvious trade. Across the world, and across the developing countries in particular, China is bridging the infrastructure gap—and in a very significant way. Its tactics are getting bigger and bolder, and so, inevitably, is the criticism China has attracted.

It's Not All Been Plain Sailing

No one can say for sure how long China's onslaught on global commodity markets will continue. But a shortage of cash won't be what slows the campaign down.

By 2011 China's foreign exchange reserves—the largest in the world—had surged to over US$3 trillion. Parts of China's vast portfolio have grown at 15 percent year on year and earned as much as US$1 billion dollars a day. As of 2011, the financial exposure in China's portfolio breaks down roughly as follows: over US$1 trillion parked in US government bonds (around 90 percent of China's US investment), some US$200 billion earmarked for other US investments, another US$100 billion in US equities (which enable China to secure ownership stakes in companies), and the balance spread liberally across the rest of the world. Money at that scale is as certain to attract enemies as it is friends, and throughout China's global rush for resources it has been accused of many things by international business people, policymakers, and media commentators—recklessness and unreasonably overpaying for assets being among the most common charges.

The China investment tracker follows not only contracts that close successfully; it also keeps a record of "troubled investments"—deals that have been canceled or whose terms have been substantially altered. Between 2005 and 2009 fifty-six deals totaling US$140 billion were rejected. Despite its progress in global space, it's not been smooth sailing for China's accumulation campaign.

US politicians halted a 2005 attempt by CNOOC (a Chinese oil conglomerate) to buy Unocal for US$18 billion, and a 2008 bid by Huawei (a Chinese information and communications technology solutions company) for a US$600 million stake in 3COM (a US digital electronics manufacturer subsequently acquired by US Hewlett-Packard in 2010).

International organizations such as the International Monetary Fund (IMF) and World Bank have also intervened in a number of China-related transactions, particularly as they pertain to African countries. A US$3 billion infrastructure-for-minerals agreement between China's Ex-Im Bank and the Democratic Republic of Congo (DRC), for example, was scrapped in 2009 after the IMF objected that the agreement would have a negative impact on the DRC's overall debt level. After much back and forth, the Chinese capitulated, caving to the IMF's demands to renegotiate the investment from an original plan of US$9 billion down to US$6 billion.

Transparency—or its lack—has been an issue with Chinese trades as well. Every day many hundreds of China-related transactions are entered into without public knowledge. These "over-the-counter" or off-exchange trades (i.e., trades that do not occur on formal exchanges) enable trading of stocks, bonds, commodities, foreign exchange, and their derivatives directly between two parties. In contrast to trading on future or stock exchanges, where the trades are (mostly) visible to all, in off-exchange trades the pricing is concealed—even though these trades have an impact on broader market pricing and other assets. There are also transparency concerns beyond pricing issues. Often there is little information on the duration of Chinese deals, or how and why the terms are negotiated as they are—even though these factors play into the broader market. Nevertheless, because of their size and because it's China, there are always attempts to reveal the details of China's commodity deals even when they are ostensibly private.

As a matter of principle, off-exchange, or private, deals are just that—private, concluded without the peering eyes of outsiders. In practice even these types of deals are monitored and subject to regulatory approval, often in the host country as well as China. But given the scope and scale of China's involvement in the global commodity area, there has been a (largely uncoordinated) demand from traders, international policymakers, local governments, and local populations in commodity-rich countries for details of deals to be disclosed.

China is also accused of overpaying for commodity assets—way above any market price that the market might deem to be fair value. Excessive payments and massive premiums place assets out of the reach of would-be competitors and ensure that China gets the spoils—at all costs. In the case of the China-Russia oil swap noted earlier, estimates of the deal suggest that the Chinese paid around US$35 per barrel (for Russian oil in the ground), whereas the market price of a barrel in the ground hovered around US$10. (Above ground the price was closer to US$65.)

At the broadest level, and perhaps most ironically given its own history, China has also been accused of neocolonialism—of executing a strategy that is merely less virulent than the colonial campaigns of days gone by. However, whereas past colonial campaigns are noted for their relatively few benefits that accrued to the locals, the Chinese approach differs in that there's something in it for the sellers.

In a March 2010 presentation entitled "International Operation of Chinese Enterprises," Li Ruogu, the chairman and president of the Export-Import Bank of China, agreed that his nation's resources campaign has features of past international forays, but he also noted important differences. For the nineteenth-century colonial powers, international trade took precedence over investment. China, he contended, has cooperated with other developing countries based on the principle of equality and mutual benefit, and it followed the market rules to acquire resources. In Africa, in particular, he stressed how China's entry into the market has broken the Western countries' long-term control over the resource exploration and international resource pricing, thereby enabling the continent to sell its energy at market price for the first time ever. Chairman Liu's comments were polite but far from apologetic: China, he said in essence, plans to achieve its global commodity, trade, and economic ambitions in the most congenial way, and it is willing to pay a lot of money to make a success of it.

One does not have to accept that China's motives are anything other than to look after China nor dismiss the possibility that there is potential for abuses, including propping up of undemocratic regimes, to conclude that China's resource campaign is, on balance, a good thing. Whether it's much-needed investment, job creation, or trade, hundreds of millions of people across the globe are in desperate need of exactly what China is happy to provide.

Do They Know Something We Don't?

A Western-educated banker took a Chinese representative to task at a global commodities conference. He publicly queried what he saw as a consistent pattern of mispricings in the assortment of assets China had purchased and in the trades in which China had engaged. He cautioned the Chinese representative about the inadequate ability of the Chinese to correctly price transactions, chiding the official that these mispricings risked overpayments by China for future transactions, which would adversely distort the broader commodity markets. He went on to showcase detailed and complicated Western models that discounted future cash flows using the appropriate market-based discount rate and spat out the model's estimate of the most accurately calculated fair value of any asset. The Chinese official sat there in dismayed silence.

There is a widely held view among traders and other international market participants that the Chinese "just don't get it," chalking up to what are seen as blatant mispricings to naïvety, ignorance, and possibly even a lack of common sense.

For the churlish naysayers of the Chinese strategy, an altogether better approach would be to engage in reverse engineering in their thinking: rather than assume that the Chinese pricing techniques are primitive, they are minded to ask themselves what would have to be true for China's pricings in its mass-commodity campaign to be right? Put another way, if their pricing were in fact sensible, what would have to be true? For one thing, the stated role of government in an economy would be a factor.

Thus, two radically different views diverge. The Chinese frame of reference is cauterized around a large, centrally planned role for the state. State-guided government agencies control businesses and deploy the factors of production—capital and labor—to meet the party's economic goals. This stance diverges from the more laissez-faire capitalist approach favored in the United States and across much of Western Europe, where, to a large extent, individuals decide how best to spend their money and deploy their labor—and this determines the landscape of commerce. It's a question of degree, of course, as there are privately owned businesses in China, and the US government does play a key role in determining ownership of business in certain sectors. Who is right?

The proper extent of government involvement in an economy has been debated for centuries. (Adam Smith's *The Wealth of Nations*, published in 1776, is an early articulation of the need to limit the role of state.) However, China's celebrated economic success and America's ongoing economic woes have brought the debate back in vogue. Here we are: two different economic slants—one largely state led, the other private-sector driven—involving two countries that could not be politically further apart. But both models are proof positive that sustained economic growth can arise from different economic paradigms and different political frameworks.

Despite the current challenges facing Western-style capitalist economies in the aftermath of the 2008 financial crisis (high unemployment coupled with high levels of disaffection, as embodied in the Occupy Wall Street campaigns), the Western-style model has been broadly successful in improving average livelihoods over many decades. But so too has the government-centric approach favored by China. The difference in political style, particularly China's state-led approach, gives China a distinct edge in accessing resources and meeting its broader economic goals, such as driving economic growth and reducing poverty. But it also goes to the heart of the reason why China appears to pay substantial amounts of money—ostensibly over value—for resource access. It boils down to China's framework, or utility function.

Here is how it works: in economics a utility function measures the satisfaction gained from consuming a good or service. More specifically, the behavior of governments (and individuals) can be explained as attempts to increase or decrease utility. Although governments may have the same utility function (they all gain satisfaction from economic betterment or improvements of their citizens), differences in the ascribed role of state mean their scope and ability to increase satisfaction will differ.

More to the point, the fact that the Chinese government has a wider role in driving the economy and determining economic outcomes means it has more levers to pull to maximize its utility function than a government with a more narrowly defined role has—as is the case of the United States, for example—and these are levers China pulls even in accessing global commodities. For instance, China's global commodity campaign is often accompanied by the deployment of Chinese hands abroad, which helps China create jobs and tackle unemployment at home.

So when China "overpays" for land, water, energy, or minerals abroad, it is essentially paying a premium price to cover access to the commodity (to meet home resource needs for economic growth) as well as other benefits, such as the reduction of unemployment (both at home and deployed Chinese workers abroad), which can propel China to achieve its developmental goals and, importantly, maintain social cohesion.

Simply put, if the Chinese government does not deliver on its economic promises—both those laid out explicitly in government speeches and work program reports and implicitly in fueling the hopes and expectations of nearly one billion people—China is likely to face political uprisings and turmoil, as witnessed in 1989 in Tiananmen Square. Such pressures can make the price "overpaid" for global commodities seem like a bargain-basement tag sale. Or put another way, no price is too large to keep the peace at home.

Reading the Tea Leaves

When it comes to China's commodity crusade, many questions remain. Take coal, for example. In September 2010 China agreed on a deal with the Russian Federation in which China would provide a US$6 billion loan to Russia—aimed at mineral exploration projects, the construction of coal transportation passages, the building of railways and roads, and the purchase of mineral excavation equipment—in exchange for the Russian promise to provide China with a steady supply of coal over the next quarter century.

In addition, China would annually import at least fifteen million tons of coal from Russia over the first five years of the twenty-five-year cooperation period. The annual coal imports would reach twenty million tons over the subsequent twenty years. As we saw in the previous chapter, China has made a similar push to shore up its copper supplies, but with copper the demand-supply imbalance is self-evident; coal is another matter altogether. China has enormous reserves within its own borders. Why, then, is it pursuing coal so aggressively?

In fact, China's autumn 2010 coal drive is just one example. According to an October 2010 GaveKal Research report, China was a net exporter of coal until 2008; in 2009 the story turned, and China recorded net imports of 100 million tons, and in the first eight months of 2010 its net coal imports were up to 145 million tons. Although these imports only make up only a small part of China's total coal demand (3 percent), they now account for around 20 percent of global seaborne coal trade.

Although this is undoubtedly good news for coal exporters like Indonesia and Australia, it is curious that China would opt to import foreign resources and save its own. Coal is not the only mineral in which such patterns seem to be in play. China's penchant for zinc imports (for which it has vast deposits) display similarly curious patterns, importing minerals when China has substantial deposits at home.

It could be as simple as China needing more coal and zinc than it is producing now, or that the process of extraction within China might be more expensive, or that the infrastructure for additional extraction needs a few years to come online. In some cases, it turns out, the Chinese buying patterns are symptomatic of falling global transport costs in the advent of technology and are an artifact of a flattening world.

Specifically, the costs of shipping goods and resources from places as far-flung as Africa or South America to China are cheaper than the all-in costs of laying down tarmac for roads or rail track to transport goods from the west of China (which is where the deposits are based) to its more economically developed and industrialized east. These all-in costs further escalate when the costs of exploration, development, extraction, and production of the respective minerals are also factored in.

For now, though, the nexus between China's aggressive coal buying, its own indigenous resources, and the world's finite supply is reflected as commodity prices in the open markets. Thus, what follows is a précis on the manner in which commodity prices are determined, particularly with China playing an ever-growing role. The intent of the next chapter, as we move into the latter part of the book, is to gain a better understanding of the pricing and inner workings of the global commodity markets, with a view of understanding how China's antics will influence the global markets and, ultimately, dictate prices in resource markets.

PART II

What China's Resource Rush Means for the World

What Have We Learned Thus Far About China and Its Commodities Push?

First, that although China occupies a vast and varied landmass, its development and economic ambitions in many ways exceed its own resources. Desertification creeps east and south from the northern reaches of the nation. Fresh water is likely to be in short supply in the not-too-distant future. Historically food self-sufficient, China became a net grain importer for the first time in 2010. The accelerating protein demands of a rising middle class are likely to exacerbate further the problems of feeding a population of 1.3 billion and rising. The housing and consumer-goods demands of that same rising middle class also mean a rising demand for energy and the raw metals and minerals that go into houses and refrigerators, large-screen TVs and automobiles.

To meet these challenges, China's leaders have embarked on a hugely ambitious program, domestically and internationally: desalination plants, pipelines, vastly expanding fleets of ocean-going transports. Like a nineteenth-century colonial power, China has ranged the world over to secure the resources needed to meet its ambitions. Unlike many of those earlier colonial powers, though, its strategy has been less to plunder the natural wealth of the countries it deals with than to strike long-range cash for commodities agreements, primarily with the "axis of the unloved"—countries and regions the West has largely ignored (Africa, Brazil, Colombia, Argentina, Kazakhstan, Mongolia, and Ukraine).

Many of China's resource plays seem perfectly reasonable. Buying a foreign mountain seems lavish in the extreme—until you stop to realize that the particular mountain in question, Peru's Mount Toromocho, contains one of the world's largest deposits of copper, a vital component of everything from wiring to plumbing and a mineral not abundant in China itself. Other resource plays do just the opposite: challenge reason. Why, when China has a hundred-year reserve of cheap coal of its own, would it be so actively importing coal?

Reasonable or not, China's resource plays reverberate greatly in the world at large. Part of that is the sheer size involved: quantities and money. The larger part, though, is the future uncertainty sown by so many of these swaps, trades, and outright purchases. What is the master plan? What effect will China's mass gathering-in have on resource prices and their availability in the short- and long-term future? These are vexing billion-dollar questions, perhaps trillion-dollar ones. But there is, in fact, an exquisite if poorly understood mechanism for measuring these issues: the global commodities market. That's where we turn next.

CHAPTER 5

A Commodity Price Précis

EACH DAY, billions of dollars' worth of commodities is traded on fifty-seven commodity exchanges spanning the globe, from Kathmandu to São Paolo, from Nairobi to Mumbai. Established in 1848, the Chicago Board of Trade is the oldest commodity exchange, but not the largest; as of 2010 that accolade goes to the New York Mercantile Exchange (NYMEX).

Commodity markets trade in agricultural products such as grains, meats, and other soft commodities, including sugar, corn, cotton, cocoa, and coffee. They are also platforms to trade energy (oil, oil products, natural gas, and power), hard commodities like minerals and metals, and exotic commodities such as uranium and emissions. Overall, exchanges do brisk business in everything from ounces of gold and tons of iron, to bushels of wheat and kilograms of rubber. As with stock markets, commodity exchanges are clearinghouses for all these resources to be traded in a transparent way, either at today's prices (i.e., spot) or as derivatives (as forward, futures, and option contracts). Even so, the distinctiveness of land and water mean they are not traded on global commodity exchanges, whereas for the most part, energy and mineral products are.

Doing Brisk Business

Although the prices of both land and water are clearly embedded in a whole range of commodities for which easily observable and transparent prices are available, such as wheat, barley, corn, sugar, cotton, gasoline, electricity, and so on, they themselves are not traded on global commodities exchanges.

The uniqueness of land (in that it is immovable and can be costly to value—you have to physically go to Argentina to gauge the quality, acidity, arability of a patch of land, whereas the metrics of a barrel of oil or a gold bar are globally standardized) means pricing and trading it tends to be localized, because there is as yet no market to set or clear land prices on a centralized global exchange. This is at least in part why trading in land tends to be fragmented, brokered by neighborhood real estate agents.

Similarly, a number of factors complicate ascribing value to water as a commodity. For instance, although bottled water is traded across international borders and offers a transparent and (theoretically) easily observable price for a unit of water, the implicit value of water itself is delinked from its price in that the value of water in sustaining life is so much greater than a market price can truly capture. What is more, water assets generally do not have clear and transferable ownership title—rarely can one individual claim rights to a specific reservoir or lake—thus making it difficult to trade water assets, as opposed to more conventional commodities.

To be traded on the global commodities exchanges, a resource has to be transferable (even if you are selling future rights to it) and transparently priced in a way that's meaningful to traders wherever they might trade around the world.

Financial Traders and Producers

Broadly speaking, commodity investors fall into two categories: financial traders and producers.

Financial traders tactically trade the market, focusing on making financial returns (by either buying or selling commodities) on a day-to-day basis with relatively short horizons. Within this category a further distinction exists between speculators or "active" investors, which include hedge funds, Commodity Trading Advisors (CTAs), and swap dealers, and index, or "passive," investors. The latter largely comprises pension funds, endowments, sovereign wealth funds, and other real money investors, each of which hold large amounts of global savings.

Beyond financial investors there is a second broad investor group, commodity producers, who adopt a more structural perspective—that is, a longer-dated view on where commodity prices will go. Companies that are involved in the extraction, development, and production of mines, farmland, and oil wells would fall into this category, as would producers and end users of the different commodities, or those who ultimately wish to take physical possession of the specific resource. These investors tend to be more focused on fundamental supply-versus-demand dynamics and, hence, are less focused on day-to-day market changes or price swings. They also tend to have direct ownership or access to the underlying asset rather than trading on market movements of commodity-related financial variables—stocks, bonds, commodity indices.[1] Put another way, they don't make their money directly through trading financial instruments in the markets but rather by profiting from the sale of the commodity itself.

A Financial Trade

Many factors drive the supply and demand—and, thus, the prices—of commodities.

Chapter 1 detailed how the speed and determination with which China pursues a kind of consumption parity with the developed world, particularly the United States, will continue to roil commodities markets. Related to this, increases in household wealth can result in consumers who make more discriminating food choices and choose higher quality protein sources, again influencing demand for certain commodities. For instance, social trends can influence end consumers to make more health-conscious choices, which in turn impacts the relative demand of one commodity over another—say, protein products like meats over carbohydrates like wheat.

Government regulation and policy interventions such as subsidies and/or taxes also can make commodities more or less expensive, as can scientific discoveries and developments that create commodities substitutes—the advent of optical fibers to replace copper, for example. And, of course, political instability, which can interrupt supply, can also influence resource prices and ultimately influence the decision of whether or not to invest in commodities.

In addition to these factors, investors look at three financial factors that drive their decisions of whether or not to buy, sell, or hold a commodity investment: carry, volatility, and correlation.[2]

Carry

Carry is the cost (or benefit) of holding an asset. A negative carry asset is one in which the costs incurred from holding it (say the cost of borrowing to buy the asset) outweigh any benefits; the converse is true for an asset said to be of positive carry.[3] Commodities are negative carry assets if the cost of holding them (say, for storage costs, insurance, security costs, or depreciation) is higher than any gain or return for holding the asset.

Since commodities do not produce interim cash flows such as dividends or interest payments, for completeness, the carry also includes a unique adjustment factor known as a "convenience yield."[4] The convenience yield reflects the benefit that, unlike other assets, it is actually possible to hold or use an underlying physical commodity (a barrel of oil or a bushel of wheat and so on).

Carry influences the slope or curvature of commodity curves. The commodity curve is simply a mapping of the price of a commodity at any given time into the future, and the shape of the commodity curve itself is nothing more than an expression of supply-and-demand dynamics prevalent in the market at any given point in time.

In general, commodities investors are looking for just what other investors are: an ascendant price curve on commodities they intend to buy or hold, and a descending one that says time to sell. Nevertheless, a specialized jargon of commodities trading exists to reflect this very fact.

Specifically, in commodity trading parlance, a commodity is said to be trading in *contango* when its spot price (the price of the commodity today) is lower than the forward price, signaling that there is ample supply in the market to meet demand. The opposite of contango is when a commodity curve is in *backwardation*. In this case the spot contract trades at a higher price to the future ones. This downward sloping, or backwardated curve, signals scarcity of supply of a commodity. In a nutshell, the distinction between contango and backwardation is crucial for market watchers to help gauge when the markets are in or approaching a stressed position.

Under contango, the future price of the commodity "rolls down" to the spot price so that the roll yield is negative—that is, the yield that a futures trader captures when the futures contract converges to the spot price. In a backwardated futures market the price "rolls up" to the spot price (a positive roll yield). A simple example of rolldown under a contango curve is if the spot price was US$60, and the future price in six months was at US$65, so that over six months the future price would roll down from US$65 to US$60, hence converging to the spot price and thus has a negative yield. In a backwardated futures market, if the spot price were at US$90 and the futures price were at US$85, the price would roll up from US$85 in order to converge to today's spot price of US$90. Basically, these curve dynamics serve as canaries in the mine to forewarn investors of tremors of oversupply or undersupply of commodities just down the road.

Volatility

Volatility also helps investors decide whether to go long (buy) or go short (sell).[5] Commodity price volatility is a function of physical infrastructure—the ease with which commodities are produced, transported, and stored—and specifically the degree to which there are constraints on these factors. In general, volatility is a positive function of price: that is, the higher the prices, the higher the volatility.

(This tends to be the opposite with equities or stocks, for which higher volatility tends to occur when equity prices collapse).

Commodity price volatility is also a function of inventories, or how much stock of a resource is available or stockpiled. In commodities, inventories are generally measured as "weeks' consumption"—an estimate of the number of weeks of consumption that existing inventories can last. When inventories fall below a certain number of weeks, it breaches a psychological barrier in which people get nervous, and this uncertainty causes volatility to increase exponentially.

Increasing demand pressures arising from emerging economies mean that physical infrastructure constraints (e.g., commodity inventories and storage capacity) are becoming more binding, making it difficult for the market to deal physically with demand shocks. Importantly, if China's aggressive entry into resource procurement were disrupting the demand-supply balance for any particular commodity, one would expect its volatility to accelerate.

Correlation

Correlation measures the degree to which two securities move in relation to each other. Perfect positive correlation implies that as one security moves, the other security will move in lockstep, in the same proportion, and in the same direction. If two securities are perfectly negatively correlated, then when one moves in one direction, the other asset moves in the opposite direction. From the perspective of portfolio diversification, the inclusion of negatively correlated assets in a portfolio can help investors achieve meaningful diversification.

In the past, commodities have been meaningfully negatively correlated to other asset classes, such as stocks, and thus a compelling addition to a well-balanced overall investment portfolio that benefits strongly from a mix of the two. However, such a harmonious balance is found mostly in an ideal world of academic models. Over time the correlation between commodities and other asset classes has turned positive—of course, to the detriment of substantial portfolio diversification. Let's consider in greater detail how this occurred.

An Illustration

A decade ago commodities were viewed as obscure, illiquid, and risky assets, left only to a handful of expert traders who truly understood the inner workings of the commodity markets. This led hedge fund manager and commodity authority Jim Rogers to quip that, "commodities get no respect." Rogers single-handedly awakened the financial industry by prophetically pointing out that one could not be a successful investor in stocks, bonds, or currencies without an understanding of commodities.

Over time commodities have evolved into an important asset class, as financial investors who traditionally maintained huge exposures in stocks and bonds now pour billions of dollars into commodity investments. In 2000 around US$6 billion worth of financial investments were invested in commodities; by 2011 these investments were close to US$380 billion—a sixty-fold-plus increase in only a decade.

Investing in commodities became lucrative as a happy confluence of the factors discussed above made for an attractive proposition. Commodities were largely uncorrelated to other asset classes (such as stocks and bonds) and thus offered diversification. Commodity volatility was low, which made Sharpe ratios—that is, the ratio of return to risk—look appealing (i.e., higher), as investors garner relatively more return for a smaller amount of risk. Finally, many commodity trades were carry-positive thanks to the backwardation of the curve, which signaled that many commodity markets were facing shortages. The backwardated curve meant, in effect, that just by holding the position and doing nothing, even the most passive of investors could make money.

Market traders are known for their herd-like behavior, meaning that they buy together and sell together billions of dollars of investment. And fueled by the promise of substantive returns and diversification benefits, the commodities trade has been no exception. *Passive financial investors* (pension funds, real money, and index investors) were early to invest in commodities, joining the producers in buying or selling commodity assets. Later, *active speculators* piled into the commodities trade, investing billions more of capital. Such was the influx of capital into commodities by financial investors that the diversification benefits that had existed began to dissipate, essentially arbitraged out by the mass volume of capital inflows. Worse still, this vast cash inflow distorted the real value of the different commodities.

From Investment Assets to Consumption Assets

The multibillion-dollar shift into commodities underscored a more fundamental, albeit subtle, psychological shift in which investors (erroneously) thought they were shifting from one investment (say stocks) into another investment (commodities), when in fact they were shifting their portfolio from *investment* assets to *consumption* assets. Moving capital away from investment assets into consumption assets is debilitating in that it reflects a reduction in the investment capital that targets important sectors, including the resource sector. Moreover, holding consumption assets is tantamount to hoarding, which reduces market liquidity.

Investment, or cash-producing, assets generate benefits in the form of future financial returns, or streams of future cash flows. Examples of investment assets include equipment, railway tracks, a company, or an idea. In the context of the resource sector, investment assets would be like investing in a mine, a productive farm, or an oil well. In each case investors put money into the assets with the expectation that at some future date they will generate a stream of cash flows.

Consumption assets, in contrast, do not produce a steady cash flow. Think of consumption assets as those from which investors seek a more immediate return or benefit through their use—say, a house or commodities that are consumed. Importantly, when investors put money in financial products like commodity indices, they are in essence putting money into a consumption asset as opposed to an investment (a commodity index is an average of commodity prices that tracks the performance of a specific "basket" of commodities). Commodity indices offer investors the possibility to garner higher returns; however, the capital invested in these financial products does not directly fund investments or investments into company projects (say, in food production or oil and mineral supply, as would equity or bond investments).

When people take their money and buy consumption assets, what they are really doing is prebuying future consumption. For example, when a person buys a house to live in, what he or she is really doing is prebuying accommodation or, put another way, prepaying, say, thirty years of future rent consumption. Similarly, when a fund buys an oil strip (an oil-linked financial investment), all they are doing is prebuying future years' oil consumption. By putting cash into consumption (financial) assets, investors inadvertently do two things. First, they celebrate a gain (improved returns) when food/commodity prices go up, when in fact society should aim to keep commodity prices as low as possible. Second, they overlook the fact that in aggregate, portfolio "wins" that occur when food/energy/commodity prices are high are actually offset by the fact that people (households, consumers, and the investors themselves) are worse off in that they have to face higher prices at the pump and in supermarkets.

Investors, of course, are always seeking a high return, but when cash earmarked for longer-term investment is diverted for immediate returns or consumption, bad things tend to happen, no matter what kind of exchange you are trading on. Witness the 2008 subprime mortgage crisis in the housing sector, in which investors diverted cash from investment assets—manufacturing or industrial corporations, say—to consumption assets, including financially constructed housing indices, which allowed people to trade housing prices without actually owning a house. In that case, when the smoke cleared, there was virtually no underlying value.

Similarly, in the commodities market, when investors chase immediate reward and ignore the means of production that creates the commodity, there's always the danger of prices rising on the back of greater fools—the idea that traders buy assets to which they do not ascribe much value but rather believe they will be able to sell on to someone else (a greater fool) at a higher price. This adds pressure for (commodity) prices to move. It would, however, be incorrect to suggest that commodity price rises (and, in particular, speculator involvement in the commodity markets) are all associated with the greater fool theory, or that speculators get involved in the financial markets only because someone else, a greater fool, will buy the asset at a higher price at some future date. In fact, more often than not, speculators, like other investors involved in buying and selling (commodity) financial assets, are focused on the fundamentals of supply and demand. Nevertheless, the danger of prices rising on the back of greater fools can lead to bubbles, which can burst and usher in periods of high unemployment, sluggish economic growth, and sizeable debts and deficits that can take decades to resolve. And critically, where commodities are involved, the underinvestment in commodity production from diverted capital leads to greater global demand-supply imbalances and general resource scarcity.

The Price of Rice in China

Over the first six months of 2011 the price of pork climbed by nearly 40 percent in China. To redress the underlying demand-supply imbalance in what is a staple of the Chinese diet, the government released frozen pork supplies from its two hundred thousand–metric ton national pork reserve. That action headed off social unrest, but, led by pork, food prices still pushed China's official inflation figures to a high of 6.5 percent in July 2011, causing the government to raise both interest rates and bank reserve requirements.

Other national governments haven't gotten off so easy. In 2007 food riots broke out in Mexico, stemming from rising prices of the corn used to make tortillas. By 2008 riots and violent unrest were registered in Egypt, Haiti, Ivory Coast, Cameroon, Mauritania, Mozambique, Senegal, Uzbekistan, Yemen, Bolivia, and Indonesia— in each case driven by food costs, which had risen by around 40 percent across the world in less than a year. All told, between 2005 and 2008 corn prices nearly tripled, rice increased by 170 percent, and wheat prices rose some 127 percent.

A number of conspiring factors drove these dramatic price movements in all cases. But the key point is that commodity prices directly impact living standards, often to deleterious effect. Food and energy price spikes can easily stoke consumer inflation. In poorer economies food and food-related purchases account for as much as half of household budgets. And food prices contribute roughly 20 percent to consumer price inflation in Western Europe and around 80 percent in countries like China.

Yet the exact factors that drive commodity prices remain a topic of considerable debate. In the main, commodity prices are influenced by a number of variables, particularly during uncharacteristic price spikes, but fundamentally, like all other goods and services, commodity prices are determined by demand and supply. Let's start with demand.

China-specific demand factors, such as the demographic headwinds in wealth and urbanization detailed in earlier chapters, put pressure on a resource—and therefore its price—if commodity production fails to match the demand. So too does concomitant consumer demand arising from the broader emerging markets such as India and Brazil.

Relatively lax fiscal and monetary policies also contribute to global resource demand and rising price pressures. In the early to mid-2000s governments across the industrialized world pursued and presided over unprecedented fiscal expansion—allowing for more money to be sloshing around the economy—and historically low interest rate environments, yielding the now well-known monstrous debts and deficits. These policies provided a surfeit of cheaply available cash across the world, and this chased the attractive propositions of commodity investments, fueled greater demand, and forced resource prices higher.

On the supply side notable linkages exist between currency price movements and the availability of commodities—metals, minerals, and agricultural products, in particular. The causality hinges on cost structure and, specifically, the relative size of the capital costs versus operating costs in the production of the commodity.

Metal and mining projects tend to have very high variable (operating) costs but relatively smaller up-front capital requirements. The variable costs are usually denominated in local currencies, whereas capital expenditures are usually denominated in dollars. As such, a weakening of the dollar elevates operating costs (as local currencies become more expensive) but has no impact on capital expenditure costs. Such cost increases put pressure on the production and ultimately lowers the supply of affected commodities. In contrast, because energy is a very capital-intensive industry with very low variable or operating costs, movements in the dollar tend to be fully priced into movements in dollar-denominated oil prices, and thus foreign exchange moves have relatively no impact on energy.

Chronic underinvestment in oil production has contributed to energy supply shortfalls globally. In particular, the inability of infrastructure investment to keep pace with the demand growth has led to persistent supply-demand imbalances across the commodity spectrum. Underinvestment in the energy sector (and agriculture as well) means increases in resource demand will eat through inventory stocks and exhaust any spare production capacity that exists, and as a result, commodity supplies are forced downward. With supply fixed and new demand coming online, commodity prices are forced higher.

Commodity supplies are also influenced by the codependence of different resources on each other. For example, agriculture supplies and prices co-move with nonagricultural prices, such as those of energy. Rising energy costs increase the costs of fertilizer, farming, and food distribution. Naturally, increased costs of transporting grain from producer to consumer translate into higher grain, agricultural, and food prices. Increased water charges and tariffs also feed into food and energy production and, hence, have the potential to hamper the supply of both resources and force prices higher as well.

Agricultural production supplies are also hampered by exogenous factors such as weather. Recurring instances of drought in Australia (since 1860 there have been nine major droughts in Australia, with the 2003 drought ranked as one of the worst) and the 1994 Brazilian frost that wiped out the country's coffee produce are classic examples of how unpredictable weather patterns can severely undermine agricultural production. Unsurprisingly, in such years, when the ratio of inventory stock to available supplies plummets, the price of foodstuffs skyrockets.

Worldwide commodity supplies are also adversely impacted by government action and interference. Subsidy programs such as the US farm bill or the analogous European Common Agricultural Policy can limit global production. Meanwhile policy interventions like the 2008 rice export ban in Vietnam or the 2010 wheat export ban in Russia place constraints on the supply of commodities into the global marketplace. Policy obstacles to the free flow of capital, labor, and technology also stymie growth in investment regardless of price or expected return, and this can create physical resource shortages over the long term—again resulting in higher commodity prices.

With such a host of variables affecting both commodity availability and prices, it would seem almost futile to attempt to pinpoint blame for shortages and spikes, but that hasn't prevented some from trying.

Speculators Speculate

In July 2011 Pope Benedict XVI proclaimed that financial trading based on "selfish attitudes" is spreading poverty and hunger, and he called for more regulation of food commodity markets to guarantee everyone's right to life. In the Pope's words: "How can we ignore the fact that food has become an object of speculation or is connected to movements in a financial market that, lacking in clear rules and moral principles, seems anchored on the sole objective of profit?"

A July 2008 World Bank report would seem to support Pope Benedict's concerns. The report found that among other factors "speculative activity" helped increase commodity prices by up to 75 percent from June 2002 to June 2008. Other estimates contend that in the run-up to 2008, speculators increased the price of oil by an average of US$9.50 a barrel.

Critics of commodity speculators point to the fact that enormous inflows of cash into any asset will have an impact on prices—especially in small markets. The fact that dramatic rises in commodity prices in the run-up to 2008 occurred at around the same time that vast sums of investment capital (including commodity-linked financial products) went into commodities further buttresses the claims that financial market players distort the shape of the commodities future curve and prices.

Competing research, though, finds no meaningful link between the "financialization" of commodities and changes in prices, concluding that commodity prices are driven by economic fundamentals of supply and demand. In a similar vein, empirical analysis from financial institutions yields more nuanced results, concluding that index or passive investors have little impact on commodity prices and more active investors or speculators have only a loose relationship with commodity prices.

In fact, despite the criticism and scorn often heaped on speculators, an argument can be made that, far from damaging markets, commodity speculators play a very constructive role in their operation. In at least two ways they maintain the efficient and orderly functioning of the financial markets and keep the commodity marketplace in balance.

First, by the very money they invest and the rapidity with which they sometimes move that money around, speculators help lubricate the markets, making it possible for commodity assets, be they barrels of oil, tons of iron, or bushels of wheat, to be more easily bought and sold, thus providing more transparency and competitive prices. This reflects the fact that speculators tend to hold a commodity position for a short period of time, for example, a matter of months, as opposed to over many years.

Second, speculators signal when shortages (deficits) or overages (surpluses) in the commodities market are likely to occur. The job of the market is to send excess supply into storage in times of surplus and draw supplies out of storage during times of relative scarcity, and this is precisely why speculators are attracted to markets in which supply-demand imbalances exist and in which the markets are not clearing. To criticize speculators for identifying supply-demand imbalances is tantamount to criticizing a thermometer for indicating that a liquid is hot.

Through their actions speculators also help guide investment decisions, ensuring that sectors or companies that require additional investment get it and that those in which there has been over-investment adjust accordingly downward. Speculator-induced higher commodity prices also encourage investments in commodity alternatives to occur so that the market is incentivized to seek other solutions to fix underlying supply-demand problems. In effect, by following the constant signals speculators send up, the market is incentivized to seek other solutions to fixing underlying supply-demand problems. As happens in equity markets, the ever-present risk that speculators would sell (or short) a commodity company's stock induces managers to constantly evaluate and optimize their capital and labor allocation so as to maintain a compelling story to investors in competitive markets.

Put another way, without speculators to flush out bad or inefficient companies, the economy is left with overvalued stocks and companies with misallocated resources. In terms of commodities, a world with no speculators would mean that we end up with artificially low commodity prices, underinvestment in commodities, and a world where the global economy routinely faces shortages rather than being induced to address the underlying supply-demand imbalances.

Hoarders Hoard

So if speculative money isn't to blame for the frequent pain caused by commodity price spikes and shortfalls, is the villain perhaps the speculators' opposite number—large institutional investors who park their money in financial instruments for long periods of time (such as commodity indices) and other consumption assets for long periods of time rather than pouring it freely over investment assets in the resource sector?

As noted earlier, although consumption assets (e.g., financial indices) enable investors to earn returns from price rises, investment assets direct cash toward companies that put their money into ideas, innovation, production, R&D, and the development of human capital in the resource sector—all of which have broad societal benefits. In other words, making an investment in the resource sector can be profitable in many ways besides commodity prices just appreciating. Absent such investment, global production, resource infrastructure, and supply of resources—food, energy, minerals— eventually slows, and commodity scarcity ensues. For society, this is the trade-off between possible short-term financial gains on your pension portfolio and food and energy shortages accompanied by higher commodity prices and worsening living standards if your capital is earmarked to consumption-like commodity investing instead of investment.

In their role as shepherds and stewards of societies' capital, pension funds and insurance companies would seem to have a binding obligation to at least consider the broader returns society garners in the form of jobs, new products, taxes, human progress, and continued supply, not just focus on near-term financial gains. After all, international agencies such as the World Bank, FAO, and World Food Programme, food companies, and governments (who aim to keep food as cheap and accessible as possible for their population) are all users and thus natural buyers of food in the future or long-dated commodity futures—as well as natural beneficiaries of investments that look beyond immediate return to long-distance rewards.

Ultimately, of course, we should all be worried about commodity price rises, whether borne of fundamental supply-versus-demand factors or influenced by the buying and selling choices of different investors. But thankfully, economies have built-in triggers to help manage the force of commodity rises.

A Delicate Balance

In practice the economic and financial markets work to ensure that the world is never out of equilibrium—at least not for long periods of time. This is often achieved by relying on factors that act as automatic stabilizers that kick in to alter demand (or supply) so that the world is forced back into balance.

Let's say the economy is booming and consumers are demanding all sorts of goods and services. In such a circumstance the increase in economic activity would have a direct effect on energy demand, so as the economy booms, oil demand also goes up. Naturally, in a world where oil supply is finite and production is capped, the effect of this spike in demand is for oil prices to shoot up very significantly.

However, the price of oil cannot keep climbing indefinitely. Even if supply can't keep up, a trigger point usually hits in which oil becomes so expensive that consumers turn to substitutes—or even do without the commodity altogether. This reduction in demand, known as demand destruction, occurs above a reservation price, the price beyond which consumers look for alternatives.[6] Over time prices must adjust and force demand growth down so that it equates to supply, and again the markets clear. That said, the trouble with relying on demand destruction to moderate price rises is two-fold.

First, it is impossible to know the reservation price *a priori*. In the case of oil and energy, as more demand has come online from

China and other emerging economies, the global reservation price has arguably risen, and it is set to rise still higher if nothing else changes. More specifically, the seemingly insatiable demand from emerging economies has meant that not only has the (global) reservation price risen (the price that people are willing to pay for energy) but also that globally the minimum price (or floor price) that consumers are willing to pay for oil has also gone up.

Second, although Western consumers want access to commodities, the fact that Chinese customers are willing to pay more for the same resources means that as the prices for commodities rise, consumers in more developed economies are the first to swap out of the commodity (demand destruction), and this can hurt Western living standards. Over the past decade as many as five million barrels per day of demand have been forced out of developed markets, and these are specifically linked to rising prices because of a global lack of supply. So, yes, the commodities markets can be self-correcting, but the balance is delicate, and the corrections do not mean a soft landing for everyone involved.

If self-correcting mechanisms fail and a managed landing is absent, carnage can ensue. In particular, through their herd behavior, speculators can contribute to speculative bubbles, in which the market price of an asset or commodity trades much higher than its intrinsic or fair value—witness the bubbles in tech stocks and the mortgage/housing market. Because speculators use borrowed money to leverage and, therefore, magnify their bets, when blowups occur, the broader economy can be detrimentally affected.

Commodity markets too are vulnerable to bubbles; indeed, some of the most spectacular bubbles of all time have come in commodities. Perhaps most famous is the "Tulipmania" that swept over Holland in the mid-1630s. In January 1637 the price of a single White Croonen tulip bulb soared 2,600 percent on the Dutch exchange—only to crash by 95 percent the first week of February, after the last great fool willing to spend the price of a grand Amsterdam canal house on a tulip bulb had finally been found.

A Message for the Commodity Markets

The question for commodity investors—China included—is how leveraged different commodity prices are to the rising global imbalance between supply and demand in land, water, the energy complex, and metals and minerals. Remember that land and water are direct inputs into food commodities such as wheat, corn, and barley, all of which are tradable on commodity exchanges and, thus, their prices of necessity reflect, to some extent, the availability of these underlying resources.

More fundamentally, if the supply-demand imbalances worsen by, say, 10 or 20 percent over the next decade, which markets will be hurt the most? And is the impact of this already being factored into always-hypersensitive commodity curves and prices? The answers to both these questions are contained in the table below.

Table 5.1 presents forecasted demand-and-supply estimates of various commodities into 2020. This is not an exhaustive list, but it does provide a snapshot of some of the commodities that face shortages and, specifically, supply-demand risks in the future. Before we get to the data and table themselves though, two disclaimers.

First, *no one* is able to predict the demand and supply (or price) of a commodity with any certainty. This is true for very large oil producers as well as the most savvy analysts and traders who have vast quantities of analytical data at their disposal. Often investors invest in commodities with massive error bars, and they can be chronically wrong for a multitude of reasons already examined, such as the unpredictable shifts in economic fortunes, weather catastrophes, and so forth. Second, demand and supply for individual commodities are dynamic, and yet the table provides only a static snapshot at one moment in time. Constantly changing commodity prices mean resource demand and supply is constantly whipsawing around and is not stationary, as the table would suggest.

Despite such shortcomings, these estimates do provide a rough indication of where some of the most knowledgeable commentators

Table 5.1 Future global commodity imbalances (for 2020)

Commodity	Some uses	Demand (2020 forecasts)	Supply (2020 forecasts)	Deficit/ surplus (2020 forecasts)	Curve snapshot (January 5, 2012)
		(a)	(b)	(c)	(d)	(e)
Copper (kt)	wiring, piping (for water, refrigeration)	34,358	18,098	−16,260	*Backwardation
Lead (kt)	batteries, weights, solders, bullets	13,712	4,205	−9,507	Contango
Zinc (kt)	galvanization and rust prevention	17,627	11,293	−6,333	Contango
Corn (1000 mt)	foodstuffs, biofuel, plastics, fabrics, adhesives	939,747	938,847	−900	Backwardation
Nickel (kt)	magnets, rechargeable batteries	2,326	2,155	−171	*Backwardation
Cotton (1000 480lb bales)	textiles (towels, denim), coffee filters, paper, tents, fishing nets	141,197	142,235	1,038	Backwardation
Wheat (1000 mt)	biofuel, foodstuffs (bread, cereal, alcohol)	715,909	717,791	1,882	Contango
Soybeans (1000 mt)	animal feed, oil	290,295	297,605	7,310	^Contango
Aluminium (kt)	packaging, transportation	72,264	134,517	62,253	Contango

*Contango at the front end; ^Highly seasonal.

Sources: Data on metals and minerals from Wood Mackenzie; Agricultural data from the USDA.

see the paths of supply and demand of certain foods, energy, and minerals playing out over time and, more importantly, frame our discourse around future commodity price movements.

The table ranks the data in order of the forecasted supply-demand imbalance—that is, from the commodity expected to have the most acute shortage (the greatest deficit, characterized by the difference between demand and supply) to the one least likely to face resource stress, and indeed a surplus (where supply outstrips anticipated demand).

Roughly at the middle is nickel, forecasted to be more or less in balance in 2020—that is, demand and supply will equilibrate. Copper, as we can see, leads the deficit projection, with lead and zinc not all that far behind. Among foodstuffs, corn shows the greatest deficit of the commodities portrayed here, but recall that corn is increasingly grown for ethanol.

On the other side of the equation a number of commodities look to be in surfeit or excess supply into 2020. For example, if the data are to be believed, aluminum, soybeans, and wheat will all post surpluses and do not appear to be at risk of shortages. The evidence suggests that producers have already reacted (and even overcompensated) to risks of global imbalances in these commodities by overinvesting and increasing production. Another explanation is, of course, that demand pressures will abate over time as the demand for certain commodities becomes satiated.

A real-life example of this is a view held by many traders that China has largely completed the rollout and expansion of its road infrastructure. With some eighty-five thousand kilometers of road network and highway (the United States has around seventy-five thousand kilometers), China's demand for iron as an input to road infrastructure is flagging and on its way down. If this were the case, the overall decline in iron demand could push iron prices downward.

From a trading point of view, traders look to go long (or buy) the commodities that are expected to be in deficit or in shortage, anticipating that the price will go up. They plan to sell (or go short) the commodities that are in surplus, expecting that a surfeit of supply will force these commodity prices lower, and they would "wait and watch" the commodities that are roughly in balance. In this latter case traders would trade more opportunistically, capitalizing on price movements as commodities swing in and out of deficit or surplus.

As any good trader will tell you, the most successful traders trade the (commodity) markets with two questions in mind: *What do I think will happen?* and *What do I think other people (such as traders, policymakers, economists, politicians, and consumers) think will happen?* The latter question calls to mind John Maynard Keynes's famous beauty contest, in which he opined on price fluctuations in stock markets that the winning strategy was for the judge not to pick the prettiest face but rather the one that best reflected who the majority of people perceived the prettiest to be.

Keynes's observation still holds. Amid the multitudinous variables of commodity trading, perception still counts a great deal, but so does mass, determination, and strategy—the mass to move the market, the determination to make it happen, and the underlying strategy that directs the mass and informs the determination. And that gets us back to China.

Beyond broader shifts in demand and supply, commodity price fluctuations will in the future come to be instigated and dominated by the global excursions of China. Its influence in determining global commodity prices is not predicated only on the fact that China wants the resources but also on how this most populous and now wealthy of the world's nations is going about getting access to them. And it is to this we now turn.

CHAPTER 6

Cornering the Market

ONCE UPON A TIME, a large, very poor but resource-rich country decided to focus on development. "We need to modernize our infrastructure, build railways, import new technologies," the government said. Soon, they had a visit from a large, wealthy Asian country. This Asian country offered them a bargain: We will give you a line of credit worth billions of dollars, and you can import our technologies. Our companies can build your ports, develop your power plants, and help you modernize your mines. You can repay us with your oil, your minerals, and access to your land. Many in the poor country were intensely suspicious of this wealthy Asian power, but they agreed to the bargain, and the work began.

One of these countries—the large poor country wealthy in oil— was China, whereas Japan was the wealthy Asian benefactor.[1] When Deng Xiaoping first proposed opening up Chinese resources to Japanese exploitation in the mid-1970s, the country was just emerging from the Cultural Revolution, and his idea was intensely controversial. But Deng prevailed, and China went on to prosper to an extent that would have been unimaginable at the time. Today, this story is still told around the world, but China is now the Asian country offering bargains to poor but resource-rich nations.

Over the past several decades China has executed a remarkably clever role reversal, in the process transforming itself from borrower to global lender extraordinaire. The most interesting aspect of this drive, however, is not just that China was successful in pursuing its goals, but also how successfully it continues to pursue its resource acquisition campaign. Simply stated, China has developed into the global price setter par excellence for numerous commodities through its specific relationships with resource-rich countries.

IOU

The biological definition of symbiosis describes a close and often long-term interaction between different biological species in relationships that can range from mutually beneficial to parasitic. The psychiatric definition is similar: a relationship between two people in which each is dependent on and receives reinforcement from the other, whether that dependency is beneficial or detrimental.

China's global commodity strategy has all the hallmarks of a symbiotic relationship: each party is dependent on the other, almost to the point of survival. China provides the cash that other countries need in exchange for the access to resources that China so desperately requires. In so doing, the symbiotic equilibrium born of commodities sets up a long-term relationship that can thrive—at least until the diminishing resources are depleted.

This kind of economic symbiosis is hardly rare. One well-known example is the so-called Chimerica relationship, by which China has lent vast amounts of money to the US government in return for virtually unshackled access to America's consumer market. As in any positive symbiotic relationship, each country gets what it wants. Washington continues to receive its vital cash loans, and China retains access to the US consumer market.

China's commodity acquisition campaign is designed to lock in countries all over the world in a similar symbiosis. Just as China was incentivized to take Japan's money in the mid-1970s to fuel its own economic success through infrastructure investment, so resource-rich nations now need China's financial investments, just as China needs to maintain the flow of those countries' natural resources.

Such dependency is strongly reinforced by the threat of financial catastrophe; breaking out of the cycle requires a country's willingness to severely damage its own economy. In the Chimerica relationship, the United States could default on its debt to China, but that would drive up its cost of borrowing substantially. America could also impose tariffs on cheap Chinese goods, an option that opens the door for similar trade barriers on American products (to the detriment of the US economy). Likewise, resource-rich economies caught up in commodity trading could restrict China's access to their assets through, say, nationalization of resources, but that course of action, even if other buyers could be found, would mean the hosts would turn their back on what is basically a guaranteed Chinese cash flow to fund projects they desperately need.

Whether the asset being traded is access to the world's largest consumer market or African nickel mines, the outcome and the essence of the trade is the same—long-term dependency in which governments get locked in indefinitely, or at least until one of the parties involved stops getting what it wants. Escape is futile, and everyone is left in hock to China. China, of course, would equally be left locked in with whatever nation controlled the asset it was pursuing if these were single-source resources, but asset sources tend to be plural, whereas China's wealth and range are, for the time being, singular.

This is not to say that countries don't try to avoid being sucked into cycles of dependency. By now this sort of trade dependency is well known, and many resource-rich nations have been grappling with the balance between guaranteeing their sovereignty and allowing the necessary investment capital to flow into their country.

Among others, the Brazilian government has been struggling with this very delicate issue, specifically with regard to granting foreign countries land access. In Brazil's case it is likely that some nationalist legal protections will come into effect before too long. Although these new regulations governing land access and tenure may take awhile to percolate through the web of special interests and competing agendas, the rules will almost certainly include more aggressive caps on foreign ownership and access to land, some limits on the uses of the land—say, between mining, cattle ranching, industry, or farming and food production—and restrictions on the allowable tenure of foreign land access and control. The increasingly strong Brazilian industrial sector has also shown rising resistance to Chinese imports as local producers have ceded market share to Chinese products. As China continues to pull out its wallet and buy up resources, such acts of resistance can be expected to become increasingly commonplace, particularly as the symbiotic partners themselves become wealthier.

The Rise of the Resource Monopolist

In July 2010 Armajaro, a London-based commodity hedge fund, cornered the cocoa market—or at least tried to.

By the end of that trading day on the London International Financial Futures and Options Exchange (LIFFE), the hedge fund had accumulated a long position on 24,100 cocoa futures contracts. Given that a single "contract" is equal to 10 metric tons of cocoa beans, the Armajaro cocoa stash was enormous, enough to fill five dry-bulk carriers the size of the *Titanic* or to make 5.3 billion quarter-pound chocolate bars. In fact, 241,000 tons of cocoa is equivalent to the entire supply of cocoa in Europe, and would have been worth close to US$1 billion at the going price of cocoa at the time. And, of course, it was a substantial proportion of the global cocoa market. By purchasing, via its long position, an amount of cocoa equal to 7 percent of annual global production—and by doing so at a time when African cocoa crops were having poor yields—the hedge fund placed enormous pressure on the supply side of an important food resource. If Armajaro simply held its 241,000 tons off the market (cocoa beans can last up to two years in storage), global demand could never be met. In this case the market reacted predictably by driving cocoa prices to their highest levels in over four decades, only to have prices slide back down a few months later on the strength of a bumper cocoa crop in the Ivory Coast. In the end, Armajaro lost money on the bet, in part because of warehousing and storage costs, which ran to as much as $10 million a month.

This wasn't Armajaro's first foray into cornering the cocoa market. With good cause, the hedge fund's principal, Anthony Ward, is known in the commodities business as "Chocfinger," after the infamous James Bond foe, Goldfinger.

Back in 1996 Ward's fund had tried to capture another corner-like position by buying up three hundred thousand tons in cocoa futures, equivalent to 10 percent of the annual crop at the time, an even bigger bet than that placed in 2010. Here, again, the commodities markets pushed back, and Armajaro ended up on the short side of the deal, but if one hedge fund can attempt such a death-defying feat, why couldn't—one might say why shouldn't—a nation with China's vast wealth try to corner certain commodity markets as well?

If China purchased enough of different commodities and accumulated high enough (or even majority) market shares, then it could strongly influence the prices of resources. But cornering a commodity market is not the only way China could gain significant control over a specific resource. The price of goods and services is set by the party—buyer or seller—that holds the most power in the relationship. China's growing role and relevance in global commodity markets means it will ultimately drive how resource prices are derived. To a large extent, this is already the case.

All Roads Lead to Monopsony

In economics a monopoly exists when an individual or enterprise has sufficient control over the supply of a product or service to significantly determine the terms, including price, under which others can have access to it.

The opposite of the better-known monopoly, where one seller faces many buyers, is a monopsony—a market form in which only one buyer faces many sellers. As the sole buyer of a good or service, the monopsonist can theoretically dictate terms to its suppliers in the same manner that a monopolist controls the market for its buyers. Monopsonists (and monopolists, for that matter) differ from the perfectly competitive markets on which the commodity exchanges are based. Under perfectly competitive markets, no single participant is powerful enough to set the market price of a homogeneous product (i.e., products that are essentially identical).

The relationship between the supermarkets and farmers is a classic example of monopsony. Think of tomato or beef production. In both instances a major supermarket chain like Wal-Mart (the sole buyer) has the market power to source products and produce from numerous farmers—multiple sellers. Other monopsonies are single-payer universal health care systems, in which the government is the only "buyer" of health-care services, or sophisticated weaponry (such as jet fighters, tanks, artillery, etc), in which only national governments can—at least, legitimately—purchase products from multiple suppliers.

China's prominent role as a buyer of resources increasingly displays monopsonistic characteristics. In fact, on China's current path it will become the buyer of choice: the "go-to" purchaser of resources, the entity that consumes the majority of global-resource output.

Déjà Vu All Over Again

In the spring of 2011 the commodity markets (and the equity market, for that matter) were enraptured by the initial public offering of the commodity trading company Glencore—thought to be an abbreviation for Global Energy Commodities Resources.

Until this time, Glencore's diversified commodity portfolio spanning soft and hard resources—agricultural products, crude oil and natural gas, coal, zinc, and so on—had been a fiercely guarded secret. Once the portfolio was opened to inspection as part of the company's public-share offering, Glencore revealed that it controlled 60 percent of the third-party zinc market (these are the transactions involving a trader or intermediary/merchant), 50 percent of copper,

45 percent of lead, 38 percent of alumina, and almost one-third of thermal coal.

Little wonder that when Glencore finally went public in May 2011, its offering was the largest ever on the premium-listing segment of the London Stock Exchange. Today, Glencore is a publicly traded company, maintaining a primary listing on the London Stock Exchange and a secondary listing on the Hong Kong stock exchange.

The breadth and extent of Glencore's ownership is an impressive display of control and muscle in the commodity markets for a company that, in its entirety, was estimated to be valued at around US$60 billion. Imagine China undertaking a similar strategy, with its vast financial reserves! Such a scenario breathes life into the possibility of the nation and its companies controlling large segments—if not all—of the world's commodity markets.

Of course, there are numerous obstacles to China's commodity market dominance coming to pass. Other countries (such as South Korea and Japan as well as the large state-owned wealth funds of Middle Eastern countries like Qatar and United Arab Emirates) and resource corporations (such as Glencore, US oil giant Exxon, or American food corporations Archer Daniels Midland, Monsanto, or Cargill) are jockeying and competing for preeminence in the resource markets too. Of course, there is also the risk of an economic slowdown in China so severe that commodity demand wanes. However, China's economic fundamentals, capital, and its leadership's desire to keep the economy progressing rapidly over time place a large discount on this scenario.

With every passing day, China is gaining market share and power, and with market power comes the increasing ability to affect the terms and conditions of exchange, so that the price of a resource will be set by the sole buyer—for all intents and purposes, China. In such a monopsonistic world, the price is no longer imposed by the market as in perfect competition; it's set by the sole buyer, and the only constraint the monopsonist faces is the limit of the market to supply. A number of factors make the likelihood of China securing significant monopsonist power in the commodities market a real possibility.

The Sources of China's Monopsony Power

Monopsonies derive their market powers primarily by erecting entry barriers. These barriers discourage potential competitors—other corporations or funds who would become buyers—from entering the market, or at least significantly hamper their ability to compete. The three major barriers to entry are policy based, economic, and legal.

A policy-based barrier exists when a corporation (or, in this case, a country) colludes with or lobbies governmental authorities to exclude competitors or eliminate competition. Already, China is viewed by many to be a monopsonist in the global coal markets.

Economic barriers include economies of scale, the cost advantages that a business obtains due to expansion, and capital requirements, the minimum capital that must be available for a company to set up shop. Clearly China has the financial muscle to meet the cash calls needed to participate throughout the commodities arena, one in which (start-up) costs can be onerous and are often followed by recurring maintenance costs such as keeping mining machinery in working order or maintaining the infrastructure to keep a farm operational. The true test of financial power is being able to keep operations running in good times and in bad—that is, throughout commodities cycles, whether prices are high or low. This challenge and the risk of substantial capital calls implicitly favor monopsonists.

To make matters worse, capital requirements in natural resource projects are associated with substantial sunk costs (irrecoverable costs such as those associated with the initial set-up and building of a mine), and these large fixed costs make it difficult for smaller players to expand, let alone enter the sector in the first place.

China's substantial wealth means neither of these costs represents an insurmountable obstacle for its resource plans.

A related economic barrier that arises from a monopsony/monopoly industry structure is the economies of scale earned from the declining financial costs over a large range of production. To the extent that China can be characterized as a near-monopsonist (given its significant representation in the commodity-buying sphere), these economies-of-scale benefits will accrue to China too, raising the entry barrier to would-be competitors. What is more, as detailed earlier, the Chinese government's subsidizing of global commodity ventures for state-owned or state-favored companies results in considerably lower costs than those of their competitors. In practice, this costing structure means state-owned Chinese entities have a close-to-zero cost of capital.

Together, China's broader benefits and subsidized cost regime make its companies' costs submarket—lower than the costs non-Chinese countries or companies and individuals would face in the financial markets. Thus, the massive presence of Chinese companies in commodities markets tends to distort readings from standard, Western-style financial valuation models, making Chinese projects look uneconomical and thus unattractive to competition. Viewed through the Chinese prism that values and supports investment in commodities beyond simply gaining profitable access to the resource, deals have a lower funding hurdle to clear. Simply put, and as mentioned earlier, the Chinese ascribe value where others see none.

Invariably, the sheer size and enormity of China's buying power today coupled with its illusionary zero cost of capital renders most potential competition impotent. Over time, as China is perceived as the only one in the game—certainly where commodities are concerned—its costs of chasing deals decline. With a declining number of buyers offering competitive prices, sellers will line up to do business with China as the first buyer of choice—and not the other way around. When that happens, monopsony becomes very profitable.

Is China Dumping?

The lowering of the break-even costs across the commodities sector is, some would say, tantamount or at least analogous to some form of dumping (more commonly seen in monopolies in the manufacturing sector).

Successful dumping occurs when the perpetrator manages to lower the costs of the sector sufficiently enough that it is no longer economical for any other rational investor to stay in the game and try to sell goods. In international trade, dumping refers to a situation in which one country exports and sells goods in another country at prices that are considerably lower than those in its domestic market. Over time the foreign imported goods can decimate the local producers, as consumers choose the more cost-effective imports over the more costly domestically produced goods. Although not directly analogous, the consequences of such trends can be seen in the United States, where the manufacturing sector has been in freefall for decades (e.g., around fifteen million US workers involved in manufacturing are unemployed, as they are unable to compete with cheaper manufactured products from the global markets led by China). Along similar lines of thinking, a monopsonist buyer—in this case China—is able to raise its bid price (the price it is willing to pay for assets, justified by the broad benefits and zero capital costs) to such high levels that others are priced out of the market.

Well aware of this tendency, the president of the Korea National Oil Corporation, Kang Young-won, in 2010 sent an unequivocal message to investment bankers pitching acquisition targets to his state-owned company: "Be mindful of competition from China and steer clear of the bigger, better-capitalized Chinese companies." In other words, don't propose projects that could lead to a bidding war with China.

China's influence has substantially impacted financial markets in the past. In 2004, for example, China managed to singlehandedly become the marginal price setter of the US Treasury ten-year bond yield, previously considered a "perfectly competitive" market.[2] Even today, the prevailing view of many market participants is—rightly or wrongly—that if China were to stop buying US government bonds, the cost of US debt would rise substantially and the dollar would weaken significantly. Why? Because China, as the lender of last resort, would be the lender no more.

The notion that prices could be determined in a monopsonistic way, with China as the single buyer, is considered sacrilege to fervent free-marketers. In this context China's efforts are seen as a clear affront to the sanctity of the capitalistic competitive economic model. China's global resource accumulation activities—its willingness to pay and overpay above "reasonable" market fair values and its eagerness to subsidize the complex and elaborate network of Chinese corporations—degrade the tenets of the perfectly competitive markets to detrimental effect: asset prices move higher—witness the soaring prices of oil and food—and resources fall into the hands of a single holder: China.

For the most part, what might be considered puritanical capitalistic outrage has little effect on China. The nation's substantial amounts of cash enable it to become the marginal buyer across a whole spectrum of commodities—the buyer who is the top bidder of assets and thus dictates the market price. There is a chance (some would say an outside chance) that perfectly balanced markets will collapse if China's ascendancy in the commodity markets continues, making China the ultimate price setter, and that China could far surpass the commodity-acquiring achievements of Glencore. China could, in fact, corner the market.

Enshrined in Law

Beyond the public policy and economic barriers, legal and regulatory frameworks can also encourage uncompetitive monopolist and monopsonist conditions within industries.

Legal rights bestowed on a corporation, an industry, or even a country offer the opportunity to monopolize a market quickly. A classic example of legally enabled monopolist control of an industry is that enjoyed by pharmaceutical companies, whose patents enshrine them as the only seller of new drugs for a specified period. The company that develops the product owns the entire market for the drug, from production to distribution. Similar situations can be found throughout the realm of intellectual property, from copyrights on books to certain kinds of proprietary technology. These exclusive rights—a kind of monopoly—are broadly designed to encourage innovation as well as research and development by rewarding inventors and creators. But because monopolies are generally considered unhealthy for the well-oiled functioning of an economy, legal safeguards are often put in place to maintain competitive industries.

Perfectly competitive markets are favored because they provide the best pricing and the greatest range of options to the consumer. Barring competition, one can imagine that a Darwinian-style market would emerge, that the strongest and fittest would survive so that the market would consist of one producer supplying (or, in the case of monopsony, one buyer purchasing) all production and, thereby, controlling and setting the price for all demand—or, in monopsony, all supply.

International commerce, antitrust regulation, and, indeed, full-blown antitrust lawsuits suggest that, left unchecked, markets may in fact trend toward monopolist equilibriums. Thus, international law seeks to police faltering markets that would otherwise make it possible for monopolistic actors to emerge. In 1998 US and European regulators separately accused Microsoft of abusing its dominant position in the computer software market to drive competitors out of business; both cases ended in significant penalties to the company. The European Union ordered Microsoft to pay nearly Euro 500 million (around US$800 million), the largest fine ever handed out by the EU at the time, as well as granting Microsoft no more than 120 days to divulge its computing information. The fines on Microsoft and the larger legal framework behind them are built on assumptions that markets naturally trend toward monopolies, yet ironically, as we'll see in the next section, these rules and regulations might actually enable China in its quest to control the commodities market.

A Legal Vacuum

Many countries' antitrust rules are specifically designed to regulate corporate activity, but there is scant antitrust legislation that applies to global sovereign government-led pursuits. In other words, many of the market protections erected to stop any one entity from gaining a stranglehold on an industry don't apply to many Chinese commodity incursions. In fact, by strictly regulating corporations while leaving government-led pursuits with a free hand, China is aided by the prevailing international legal environment. By eliminating some of China's likely competition in acquiring resources, these regulations inadvertently help China become the price-setting monopsonist in the global commodity industry. China's command in land and agricultural plays, whether in Brazil or across Africa, are one case in point. Though an obvious legal vacuum exists, global policy making has been ineffective, partly due to inaction, partly due to inadequate attention, and partly due to powerlessness.

Leading international agencies such as the World Bank do publish work on the state of the commodity landscape, and national governments set policy around their individual needs and production, but despite the potentially devastating consequences of unsatiated commodity demand in a world of more binding resource scarcity—including the likelihood of resource-based conflict across the globe—no coordinated global body deals singularly and comprehensively with the legal and policy issues related to resources.

Ad hoc decisions by individual governments may block China's enthusiasm—for example, the United States blocking Chinese purchases—but barring the creation of a coordinated, universally subscribed-to legal framework to govern the behavior of the Chinese state, most policymakers will continue to adopt a national rather than global purview, unprepared for the very real cross-border commodity risks that will be faced in years to come.[3] Meanwhile, China will likely continue to increase its market share, access, and control in land acreage, energy, and minerals worldwide.

A Legal Minefield

China's pursuit of a controlling interest in commodity markets may represent a new global challenge, but the lack of any forceful international law governing this murky area is not new.

For example, it is beyond question that if the Organization of Petroleum Exporting Countries (OPEC) member nations were private companies, they would have been fined heavily and/or had their executives put in jail in the United States or the United Kingdom for collusion in oil production, influencing prices, and violating antitrust rules. Instead, US courts have refused to exercise jurisdiction over OPEC. The US Congress attempted to remedy the situation by passing the No Oil Producing and Exporting Cartels Act of 2007 (the NOPEC bill). But for reasons of international public policy, President Bush vetoed the measure.

What was really telling, though, was the statement the White House issued after rejecting the bill. "This bill has the potential to lead to oil supply disruptions and an escalation in the price of gasoline, natural gas, home heating oil and other sources of energy," the statement noted. Furthermore, "The administration supports a market-based international energy trade and investment system. However, the administration believes that the appropriate means for achieving that objective lies in diplomatic efforts by the United States with the countries involved in that trade, rather than lawsuits against those countries in U.S. courts." Finally, noting that approving NOPEC would trigger retaliation against the United States and hurt the country's oil supply, the White House offered that "such a result would do little to achieve a free market in international trade in petroleum, would substantially harm other U.S. interests abroad and would strongly discourage investment in the United States economy."[4] In short, the legal challenge may be valid, but the United States would rather talk in back rooms with the heads of the OPEC nations than get caught in a nasty trade war with the world's largest block of oil producers.

China can reasonably infer a similar takeaway.

Although a credible charge against the Chinese could be brought on antitrust grounds, given the significant space China now occupies in commodity markets, the OPEC precedent suggests that such a case is unlikely. And, in fact, the weight that China has to throw could mean that an existing global legal framework that specifically addressed China's aggressive incursions into commodities might remain unenforced. Ultimately, exceptions in trade negotiations are made all the time, with political horse-trading in investment contracts (directly in factories or bonds), trade agreements, and even commodity deals all on the table.

Despite the low likelihood of successful lawsuits being brought against China today, the nation's approach to competing internationally is rapidly evolving with the assumption that over time competition and antitrust law will almost certainly apply to resource transactions in a similar way as they do to industrial transactions (like the fines on Microsoft). In recent years China has seen some of its leading corporations come under the scrutiny of antitrust regulators worldwide. In 2003 China's TCL and France's Thomson combined their TV and DVD businesses to form the world's biggest television maker. Seven years later Chinese company Zhejiang Geely Holding Group acquired the Swedish brand Volvo for US$1.8 billion purchase. Though both actions were ultimately allowed, the Chinese leadership was reminded that more aggressive and broader antitrust regulation aimed at similarly large commodity acquisitions couldn't be far behind. After all, unlike industrial transactions, China's commodity campaign has more far-reaching consequences for all consumers in that they impact the global price of resources and ultimately the costs of goods and services for the average consumers; politicians wherever they might be, will sit up for this.

China's approach to commodity transactions is certain to change as the attitudes of both buyers and sellers change. To date, China's resource campaign has been advantaged in part by flouting the rule of law, especially as applied to lesser-developed resource-rich countries, where enforcement is underfunded, centralized in the hands of few, or virtually nonexistent. For example, the din of vocal objections is increasing both to Chinese companies and Chinese workers operating in some African countries. As public dissatisfaction meets China's expanding demand for resources, the operating landscape is bound to change, with some host nations placing greater demands on China and limiting the country's flexibility.

Similar dynamics will encourage a different relationship between Chinese buyers of commodities and the laws of their host nations. Buyers will increasingly realize that they must take account of both Chinese and foreign competition law as well as manage and respond to sensitivities when making investments abroad. More generally, this signals that as China gains more global deal-making experience in the commodity space and its skills are continually elevated to world standards, the chances are that China's aggressive and opportunistic investment approach in global commodities will be honed and evolve into a more mature model. A model that has more elements of transparency—at a minimum transparency in the pricing of the transactions and other terms of the trades. Of course greater transparency on the price of commodities and the demand-and-supply dynamics that are moving these prices is always a good thing.

Whatever the case, China's aggressive campaign continues to increase, as does its influence on prices and how the world as a whole interacts across the entire commodities space. The trouble is that in a world of mounting resource scarcity, the leverage of the rest of the world on China is declining.

CHAPTER 7

Meddling in the Markets

THE NOBEL LAUREATE ECONOMIST Amartya Sen once observed, "There is no such thing as an apolitical food problem." His statement, at least in part, reflects the fact that governments around the world try to prevent crises—like food shortages—with a wide variety of policy levers that influence both demand and supply. In China, for example, the one-child policy helps reduce overall demand for food.[1] Meanwhile, through agricultural protection via subsidies, the United States and Europe encourage greater food supply. Each year, these governments (and many others) earmark hundreds of billions of dollars for agricultural subsidies that restrict food imports and provide financial support for domestic farmers to produce more food, often far in excess of demand.

Although the Chinese state is making aggressive moves within global commodities, it's not alone in meddling with the resource markets. The net effect of this meddling is that government actions join the ongoing depletion of natural resources in having significant consequences on commodity supply and demand.

The debate on the optimal economic role of the state is as old as economics itself. The most famous recent episode follows the multi-trillion-dollar interventions to stem total economic collapse in the wake of the 2008 financial crisis. That said, where government involvement is debated, it's important to understand how a credit crunch fundamentally differs from a commodity crisis. In any market, but particularly in publicly traded markets, regulators are duty bound to reduce the probability—or, at least, limit the damage—of market failures. This is no mean feat. Consider the workings of a commodity market against that of the credit market.

Back to Basics

Imagine that a spell of bad weather wipes out a whole potato crop, dramatically reducing the supply. The human cost could be devastating—the nineteenth-century potato blight in Ireland saw crop failures of up to 30 percent, contributing to the Great Famine of 1844 to 1849 in which one million people died. In market terms the collapse in available potatoes does not immediately change the demand for potatoes, so the price of potatoes increases upward to adjust to the new supply-demand equilibrium. The rise in potato prices then attracts and encourages other potato producers (wherever they may be, at home or abroad) to pick up the slack in supply by growing more potatoes. Over time, as the supply of potatoes increases, the market price readjusts and settles closer to the original supply-demand balance and price point. In functioning markets, such as commodity markets, this self-correction happens naturally, so government intervention is not necessary to fix the market; in fact, government action could be harmful. For example, were the government to step in and itself source potato supply, this intervention could permanently discourage would-be commercial potato farmers from getting involved.

Now consider the credit markets. Almost all banking crises begin when banks experience an increase in defaults as their borrowers are unable to keep up with their debt repayment obligations. The 2008 financial crisis followed exactly those mechanics when subprime borrowers began to default on their loans. Suddenly, the highly leveraged banks—many which also had borrowed the money they lent—owed large sums of money to their depositing customers, who in turn owed money to other banks, thus escalating the problem in a decidedly unvirtuous circle. The delicately interlinked nature of credit markets meant the speed and scale at which the defaults occurred had dramatic consequences not just for banks but also for the world economy as a whole.

In March 2007 US subprime mortgages were valued at around US$1.3 trillion, with over 7.5 million first-lien subprime mortgages outstanding.[2] By July of that same year subprime-type mortgages represented only 6.8 percent of outstanding loans, but they represented 43 percent of foreclosures, and by October around 16 percent of subprime adjustable-rate mortgage loans were either three months delinquent or in foreclosure proceedings—triple the 2005 rate. The next January the delinquency rate had risen to 21 percent, and by May 2008, it was 25 percent. The consequence: by the middle of 2008 major banks and other financial institutions around the world were reporting losses of almost US$500 billion.

Ultimately, without the repayment money coming in from their subprime borrowers, many banks did not have enough cash to run their operations. As pressure mounted to keep their operations afloat, banks began to lean on customers in hope of recouping at least some portion of the loans they had extended. These customers responded to the pressure from their banks by withdrawing their cash deposits in other banks, which led those banks to go to their depositors, with the carry-on effects wreaking havoc on banks, households, corporations, and even governments. Although crises in the commodity (potato) market and the credit market can both wreak irrevocable damage on people and whole nations, credit markets have unique characteristics that set them apart from commodity (as well as other) markets.

For one thing, the credit markets tend to have repeat crises, whereas other markets do not. In *This Time It's Different: Eight Centuries of Financial Folly*, Carmen Reinhart and Kenneth Rogoff count 235 financial crises dating from England's fourteenth-century default to the recent US subprime financial crisis, covering sixty-six countries in Africa, Asia, Europe, Latin America, North America, and Oceania. Their analysis shows that credit crises have similar origins and characteristics.

Additionally, credit markets are the lifeblood of not just one country's economy but also the global economy, with significant knock-on effects on other industries and sectors worldwide. Specifically, these networked interdependencies mean credit-market failures feed into the broader economy and can expand beyond sovereign borders; they have the tendency to be significantly amplified and magnified, particularly in an interlinked globalized world. This is why credit-market failures carry with them "systemic risk"—the risk of collapse of the entire financial system or, as was witnessed in 2008, the whole global economy.

Finally, credit markets are not self-correcting in the same way commodity markets are. (A potato crop fails in one country, and farmers in another change to potatoes to take advantage of the shortfall in supply.) Thus, the government must step in to avoid very detrimental consequences.

These unique characteristics of credit-market crises are why there are two incontrovertible instances when government intervention in an economy is warranted: (1) stopping criminal activity and (2) resolving failures when markets fail to clear, particularly when problems in one sector could undermine the broader economy.

Because the question of government intervention in commodity markets falls outside these criteria, state-sponsored action by China (or any other nation for that matter) in the broader commodity markets—and the possible responsibilities therein—leads to much more complex questions.

Government Intervention

In September 2010 the *Washington Post* ran an astonishing story. The US Department of Defense, according to the report, was attempting to buy the entire first-print run—some ten thousand copies—of a memoir penned by a former Defense Intelligence Agency officer so that the book could be destroyed. Although the details of this government intervention remain scant, it was a stark reminder that the specter of government is ever present. More fundamentally, whether it's state-led China in the commodity markets or the ostensibly laissez-faire US government managing literary outputs, governments can and do act. Books, of course, are one thing, and commodities another, but whether the property being protected is intellectual or physical, the motivation for government intervention takes two basic forms.

First, nations may intervene with *political* considerations in mind, such as protecting state secrets or the country's own food supply. Creating food self-sufficiency—even if buttressed by market-distorting policies—ensures that a country is not left vulnerable to food shortages if the source country's ability to produce and supply food becomes restricted by, say, a natural disaster or war. In this vein Russian premier Vladimir Putin imposed a 2010 ban on grain exports to preserve his nation's domestic food supply. In 2008 China, India, Pakistan, Cambodia, and Vietnam curbed rice exports to ensure there was enough to feed their citizens. The political rationale for intervention can also extend to matters of national pride and ownership: the idea that the natural resources with which a country is endowed belong to that nation and its people, not to individuals or corporations.

The state also intervenes in commodity markets for *economic* reasons, such as protecting the jobs and incomes of domestic farmers. The subsidies with which the United States and Europe prop up their domestic agriculture are economic policies fashioned to cajole their citizens to prefer nationally produced goods and services over foreign produce. But even beyond trade policy distortions such as subsidies, tariffs, and currency manipulations are situations in which governments take explicit stakes in their resources. A classic example is the attention nations tend to heap on oil. Because of the commodity's value and importance within the global economy, oil is frequently controlled by state companies. In fact, measured by reserves, the thirteen largest oil companies in the world are owned and operated either partially or wholly by governments. State-owned companies such as Saudi Arabia's Saudi Aramco, the National Iranian Oil Company, Petróleos de Venezuela (PDVSA), Russia's Gazprom and Rosneft, the China National Petroleum Corporation, Malaysia's Petronas, and Brazil's Petrobras control more than 75 percent of global oil reserves and production.

As a result, these countries are able to influence directly the quantities of both supply and demand volumes throughout the broader market.

In China three key state-owned actors participate in the oil market: Petrochina, Sinopec, and CNOOC, with the latter primarily focusing on China's offshore oil assets. Although China is also home to over six hundred private oil companies, these "Big Three" have the lion's share of the activity in China's energy realm. Between them these government-controlled companies sell, refine, produce, and distribute the vast majority of the oil in China.

Massive oil reserves are another government-managed mechanism that can influence energy markets. The US Strategic Petroleum Reserve, for example, is one of the largest in the world; with four sites, the caverns have a capacity of 727 million barrels. Other countries with oil reserves include South Africa, Kenya, and Malawi in Africa; India, Thailand, and South Korea in Asia; and many countries in the Middle East. In March 2001 the International Energy Agency (which includes the United States, the UK, Japan, and many of the major European economies) mandated that all twenty-eight members of the group have a strategic petroleum reserve equal to ninety days of the prior year's net oil imports for their respective countries. The European Union also mandates specific requirements for its member countries' strategic reserves. According to the US Energy Information Administration, approximately 4.1 billion barrels of oil are held in strategic reserves around the world, of which 1.4 billion are government controlled.

The establishment of physical strategic reserves helps smooth and stabilize supply shortfalls and, thus, the gas price consumers face at the pump. This is particularly true in times of significant oil price volatility in the broader global markets. A recent case in point was in June 2011, when the United States and the International Energy Agency coordinated a move to release 30 million barrels each from their strategic reserves. This action was largely in response to significant oil price rises and volatility: oil prices were around

US$90 a barrel, and Americans were facing gasoline prices at on average above US$3.60 per gallon. The volatility was at least in part driven by the political uncertainty across the oil-producing states of the Middle East and North Africa—particularly Libya, which supplies around 1.5 million barrels of oil per day into the markets and was then in the midst of its Arab Spring uprising.

Meanwhile, recognizing that commodity resources—and oil in particular—are depleting assets, governments of petroleum-producing nations have created what might be thought of as fiscal strategic reserves in the form of sovereign wealth funds, built up with oil-based revenues. In general, the proceeds of commodity price windfalls are set aside or ring-fenced so that they are treated as separate from the regular government coffers and budgets. The Norwegian Sovereign Wealth Fund (also known as the Norges Bank Investment Management) is a good example of this. The fund has responsibility for investing the money Norway earns from its North Sea oil riches. With around US$550 billion under management in October 2011, it remains in the top-three largest sovereign wealth funds in the world. Yet the fund allows only a small proportion of its wealth to be consumed today, choosing instead to save and invest the vast proportion of the fund for future generations.[3]

Holdings in petroleum are among the best-known reserves, but governments also hoard other commodities in great quantities to ensure economic and national security at times of commodity crisis. Saudi Arabia, Russia, and Egypt, for example, all have strategic wheat reserves. And as noted earlier, China has a strategic pork fund.

Nonetheless, intervention in the energy markets can be much more insidious, with governments inveigling the oil markets at every stage of the value chain. From output (e.g., through control over licensing governments determine what and how much comes out of the ground), to distribution, to the end users and consumers and management of downstream operations, governments are involved, and to be sure, the Chinese state is involved.

The Long Arm of the Chinese State

China's energy sector operates under the broad auspices of its energy czar—the National Energy Administration (NEA). China has established a strategic petroleum reserve (SPR), a network of government-controlled bases, and a few mandated commercial entities that hold China's oil reserves. And as with other countries, China hoards oil inventories to help the nation avoid economic dislocations due to fluctuations in world energy prices. In essence, these reserves act as a hedge so that oil reserves accumulated when the world oil price is relatively low can be drawn on when oil prices are high or when oil supplies are relatively scarce in the international markets. The NEA takes advantage of low global energy prices to replenish and increase the oil in reserves.

China has aggressively bolstered its oil inventories via the SPR system ever since the 2004–2007 surge in world oil prices left the country seriously lacking in energy. That price surge laid bare the vulnerability within China's economic plans and development agenda, which are subject to the whims of the international energy markets, leading directly to efforts to significantly expand reserves so that China would not be disadvantaged when compared to other major oil-consuming countries.

China will have built eight new strategic petroleum reserve bases by 2013, adding to the currently existing four. In total, this will increase China's strategic crude reserve capacity to nearly three hundred million barrels. More generally, China's planned trajectory of state reserves will leave its SPR with nearly five hundred million barrels, or about a fifty-four-day supply, by 2016. In addition, China has commercial storage capacity of around three hundred million barrels of crude oil and is building an eighty-million barrel refined oil stockpile. In total, this would equal about a ninety-five-day supply. To put this in context, during the 2004–2007 period China's national oil inventory covered only twenty-one days of its economy's needs, as compared, say, to Japan and the United States, which both had enough reserves for one hundred days.

To say that energy concerns are an important strategic concern for China is an understatement. As the world's second-largest consumer of oil, China relies on imports for about half of its oil needs—China's net oil imports in 2010 were at 4.8 million barrels per day, expected to increase to 5.9 million barrels per day in 2012. Even still, China badly needs energy. The NEA planned to ensure a two hundred–million-ton domestic annual oil output from 2009 to 2011, but even with this in store, the trend of growing dependence on imported oil will remain. In fact, China is projected to continue to be importing up to 60 percent of its oil into 2020, and this could rise to as much as 72 percent by 2035.

Increasing strategic reserve capacity is clearly a common governmental response to volatile oil price and supply; however, there are other ways in which the Chinese government actively manages the oil market, going beyond the manipulations that other developed economies see as necessary. China places both caps and controls on energy prices. This technique allows China to set the price of oil facing consumers at the pump—and falls in line with the general strategy of the Chinese government to have a very visible hand in everything.

Likewise, state-owned companies such as China National Petroleum Corporation (CNPC) and Sinopec control oil-importing licenses with the aim of ensuring an orderly oil market.

The official view, articulated by Tong Lixia, a Ministry of Commerce researcher, is that "if import licenses are issued to private companies and there is no proper management, that could lead to speculation and oil market disorder and even threaten national security"—justification for government intervention if ever there was one, assuming, of course, that the premise is accurate.

The end result of all this government interference—whether through subsidies, tariffs, or hoarding—is substantial distortions of prices, supply, and demand, all of which ultimately hamper the ability of commodity markets to work efficiently. In effect, market distortions—whether they involve China's collecting resource assets into a vast global portfolio and ostensibly cornering many parts of the commodity markets, or Western economies imposing quotas and subsidies in the agricultural or energy markets—result in the same outcome: an assertion of dominant control in the commodity markets, and this can be disruptive to global consumers.

True, many governments are guilty of these distorting activities to some degree or another, but plenty of commodity market traders argue that the US and European interventions do relatively little that impacts investors' ability to be punished or rewarded for reading fundamental market signals; instead, their interventions tend to be known quantities with a lot of visibility and communication regarding the time frame within which policies are being implemented and executed. There is, in short, a fair degree of transparency in the interventions of the United States and Europe.

In contrast, so much uncertainty surrounds the Chinese resource mission—when China buys, how it buys, and when it stockpiles—that many market participants find themselves in a haze in which correctly predicting the impacts of Chinese behavior is enormously risky. (Conversely, if read correctly, these bets on murky situations can generate real and significant financial returns.)

Do as I Say, Not as I Do

Beyond manipulating pricing (via subsidies and so on), influencing output by state-led rationing (think of the OPEC cartel), and hoarding inventories, countries also manage their access to resources by simply locking out other countries or international corporations. Banning foreign agents from access is an altogether more aggressive approach for maintaining commodity control, but it is also a technique used by governments around the world.

For example, between 1988 and 2008 the US government rejected nearly two thousand proposals for foreign entities to acquire businesses domiciled in America. That's one hundred each year— nearly two rejections a week. By comparison, only two transactions have been rejected by Canada's Foreign Investment Review laws since its inception in 1973. In 2008 the Canadian authorities nixed the proposed acquisition of MacDonald Dettwiler and Associates (MDA) by US-based Alliant Techsystems Inc. Then, in November 2010 the Canadian government ruled against mining giant BHP's proposed US$38 billion acquisition of Potash Corporation. Both of these rejections were arguably in the national interest. MDA is an industrial company involved in highly engineered materials used in defense security and aerospace, and Potash is the world's largest fertilizer company, with important commodity production operations in phosphate and nitrogen.

In the United States the Committee on Foreign Investment in the United States (CFIUS) reviews the national security implications of foreign investments in US companies or operations. As with the Canadians—only far, far more frequently—a large number of the US denials are in the area of national security and commodity resources, such as the failed 2005 attempt by Chinese oil conglomerate CNOOC to buy Unocal for US$18 billion. Although Chinese companies are not the only groups denied access to and control of US-based operations, as concerns about China's aggressive moves into markets and relatively opaque business practices grow, the country does seem to be bearing the brunt of not just US but also international reservations. Indeed, as detailed earlier, China's approaches have been snubbed not only by host countries like the United States but also through opposition from third parties such as the IMF.

Possession Is Nine-Tenths of the Law

Commodity-based deals have a nasty reputation of falling prey to time-inconsistent policies from host governments. One minute they woo you; the next minute they think nothing of reneging on a deal.

Within commodities markets specific—and notorious—issues of access and possession repeatedly flare up. Host governments have a resource trump card to play when turning up the pressure on foreign investors: it is much more expensive—and often impossible—for companies to relocate their mining operations or oil drilling than other industrial operations like, say, shoe production. Because almost all resources are either inside (minerals, oil) or directly tied to the ground (lumber, agriculture), extraction operations can easily fall prey to host governments determined to change, say, profit-sharing arrangements. And there's the perennial threat of outright expropriation of a commodity-producing operation.

Some of the countries with the biggest mining deposits (e.g., the Democratic Republic of Congo) and largest prospects for oil (e.g., Venezuela) have shown no reservation about—with little or no notice—tearing up a bona fide contract and reassuming ownership of an asset. If anything, on a number of occasions they have shown an outright propensity to renege on deals. Never mind the lost investment capital laid down by investors and (outside) corporations. Never mind job losses from those working in the mine. Within commodity markets policymakers can and do change their minds on a whim.

The questions of energy and mineral ownership and access are even trickier than control issues around water and land. The latter are, to a large extent, resolved by borders and geopolitics. Resource ownership for tradable commodities such as oil and many minerals are instead embedded in publicly observable prices. In fact, price information contained in publicly traded commodity markets is a good guide to highlight the tension between outright ownership (say, as stipulated by contract decree) and only nominal control of a natural resource asset (where only rights for access and some use of the asset are conferred).

This policy uncertainty almost always raises the cost of capital and invariably reduces investment, as some potential investors choose not to put their money down on too risky a proposition. As a result, companies that operate in areas of extreme uncertainty have share prices that trade at a discount or seem persistently depressed—regardless of the quality and quantity of the underlying asset or deposit. Many of the mining companies that operate in the

Democratic Republic of Congo would fall into this camp. To make matters worse, the uncertain political environment means that often these companies have to fund themselves with upfront (more expensive) equity capital outlays, as few people would ever lend to them in the form of (cheaper) debt.

In environments of economic stress and political uncertainty (which can work in tandem—the more economic problems, the greater the political volatility), the cost of capital sometimes rises to such an extent that the public debt markets are slammed shut. If and when the surrounding uncertainties are resolved, the share price of the company rallies higher, becoming much more reflective of traditional factors such as management, cash flows, asset quality, and so on that are associated with the asset.

Ownership versus Control

One way to make sense of these ownership-versus-control issues surrounding investments in oil and minerals is to envision a bell curve–type distribution. An extreme at one tail of the distribution occurs when commodity prices are notably high, as when the oil price per barrel hovered around US$145 in July 2008, as compared to a US$20 per barrel average in the preceding decades. In this situation the risk of expropriation is considerable, with ownership of the asset leaning toward the government. Increased government involvement can also take the form of higher royalties or taxes on the asset or dictating the size and direction of sales. For example, emboldened by high prices, Venezuela's president Hugo Chávez routinely threatens to halt exports to the United States from his nation's state-owned oil company, PDVSA, despite the United States being Venezuela's biggest oil-trading partner.

The extreme other tail of the bell curve occurs when market prices collapse, as on Monday, October 19, 1987—known as Black Monday—when stock markets around the world shed enormous value in a very short time. The Dow Jones Industrial Average, for instance, fell over five hundred points (or nearly 23 percent) over a matter of hours. In the analogous commodity scenario, investment is likely to fall as companies already in the sector can no longer break even and instead shut down mines and oil fields—sometimes permanently. In this extreme, as with the one described above, the end result is the government assuming ownership of the underlying asset, but for entirely different reasons.

This latter scenario played out in Zambia in 2002 when the slump in copper prices rendered the operations of the venerable Anglo American company uneconomical and prompted it to quit its Zambian operations, leaving the mine in government hands. Eventually the copper assets were privatized and sold to private companies that resumed production, although, through its own investment vehicle, the government of Zambia retained a minority equity stake in many of the mines.

Another way of making sense of resource-rich host-government behavior is the logic of the options market. Options are financial instruments that grant the buyer of the option the right—but not the obligation—to buy or sell an underlying asset, whereas the seller of the option grants the right to trade (buy or sell) the asset at a given price in the future. Because they own or hold the rights to the mine, the oil well, the land, and so forth, governments are in finance parlance, "long" the underlying asset. When commodity prices soar, the demands of the host government on an asset, such as tax revenues and higher royalties, can rise exponentially. At extremes these demands result in expropriation or nationalization of the asset. In market terms this would be like exercising their long-call option on ownership (as the government gains as the commodity price shoots up).

Conversely, when commodity prices plummet and companies struggle to break even from operating their business, they will likely "put" back the asset to the government—that is, essentially short a put option. In this case the government ends up owning a greater amount of the asset as its value plummets, and the company, in essence, "wins" (i.e., limits losses) because it can cease operations and walk away from the asset as commodity prices fall. Again, the ownership of the asset falls back to the government, which is forced to take over the mine, oil well, or farm in order to help keep local citizens employed in the abandoned project.

In summary, when commodity prices are very high or relatively low, the government assumes ownership and control of the underlying asset. When commodity prices trade within a moderate range, investors assume at least some (nominal) control over an asset because there is not significant upside potential or downside risk from commodity price shifts, as at the extremes/tails. The Chinese have played the role of both host country and foreign investor within this logic.

As China has rapidly expanded as a buyer of foreign resources, it also has expanded its access to resources over a diversified portfolio of countries, a strategy to minimize the risk of commodity-supply shocks should the behavior of a host government change. The Chinese have also attempted to reduce risk—or hedge commodity exposures—by putting in place such symbiotic structures as low-cost loans, infrastructure creation, and other inducements in return for access to commodity assets. These relationships not only benefit both parties; they also disincentivize both sides from abandoning whatever agreements exist between them.

As a host country, China has not always rolled out the resource red carpet. Although foreign companies working in the mining sector, for example, have found it relatively easy to secure exploration licenses when the odds of striking gold are slim to none, things become tighter as the odds of a mineral discovery increase. Through the development of the mine to the production phase—when a company starts reaping rewards as it extracts and sells the asset—the rights of a foreign company to a license decline exponentially at each new step.

As with other countries, the Chinese state holds a free-call option in which its ownership rights increase as the asset value rises. The exploration costs are almost wholly borne by the foreign outfit, but once evidence emerges that minerals exist, the upside (nearly wholesale) transfers to China. This is not to say that foreign corporations do not earn anything. They do, and it's these potential earnings that incentivize foreign investors to invest in the resource sectors along with many others—banking, retail, and so forth. But these earnings are considerably lower than they might be if the Chinese government withheld smaller amounts of the windfalls.

Is this practice likely to change as China expands its already-extensive commodity profile? It's hard to imagine why China would abandon what is, after all, a global practice, but as the weight of all commodity exchanges shifts in China's favor, it just might find it tempting to increase the pressure still more on those seeking to do business within its borders.

The Limits of Capitalism

In theory, if price mechanisms are working efficiently, China's commodity crusade should leave everyone better off. Those who want the commodities the most, like China, will be willing to pay the most for them, and their bid for all manner of resources should be an economic boon for people around the globe. In practice, however, the demand for finite commodities could just as easily raise resource prices and spawn inflation that pushes worldwide living standards down.

With specific regard to China, there is another danger. As the "owner" of assets across the globe, China could become reluctant to share or sell commodities—a risk that rises as resource constraints become ever-more binding. Such a scenario almost always leads to political instability, expropriation, and even outright conflicts, as different countries fight to access resources.

The bottom line is this: from Beijing to Brussels, Washington, DC, to Caracas, and well beyond, state meddling in the commodity markets is endemic. Whatever tool of political intervention is relied upon—protectionism, subsidies, hoarding, even posturing—the result is the same: introducing uncertainty in the investment decision.

Textbooks, at least at the introductory level, enshrine the free-market interplay of supply and demand, but today the truth is that immediate natural resource dynamics have more to do with politics and politicians than economics or ideals. And China's strategy of befriending governments across the world shows just how this is done.

CHAPTER 8

The Geopolitics of It All

C HINA'S ASCENDENCY in the resource markets brings with it real and extensive geopolitical and social transformations beyond just impacting commodity prices.

This is not unusual in itself. Any rapidly growing actor—and certainly one with China's scope and aggression—will inevitably alter not just the landscape of how business is done but also how countries themselves are run. Although the political and social outcomes of China's quest may not be on its agenda *de jure*, they are most certainly on China's agenda *de facto* as an unintended consequence of China's commodity rush.

In the midst of its resource crusade China has no option as to whether it will impact issues of national sovereignty and geopolitics, just as it cannot avoid engagement with the international community or have some ramifications on, say, the labor laws and environmental policies of its host countries. But China can, to a large degree, guide the specific directions in which these changes move, and the host countries themselves can be resistant or receptive to China's impact on their internal affairs. Despite claims to the contrary, these social impacts are not universally negative.

A Wolf in Sheep's Clothing?

In June 2011, during the African Growth and Opportunity Act meetings in Africa, US secretary of state Hillary Clinton cautioned that Africa must beware of "new colonialism" and reminded the audience that "we saw that during colonial times it is easy to come in, take out natural resources, pay off leaders and leave." Though China was never explicitly mentioned, its comments were quickly interpreted as a thinly veiled attack aimed at China.

Unsurprisingly, the suggestion that China's influence in Africa could spawn a "new colonialism" was quickly met with scorn from Chinese representatives. Hong Lei, a Chinese Foreign Ministry spokesman, dismissed the remarks, saying that China has never imposed its will on African countries. Hong Lei expressed the hope that naysayers could evaluate Sino-African cooperation objectively and fairly, and he went on to stress that China was committed to respecting African countries and cooperating with them for "mutually beneficial gain." Although the press statements issued by any government, including China's, should be taken with a grain of salt, this time China's official spokesman was more right than wrong.

Sovereignty is defined as one country having supreme, independent authority over a geographic area, region, or predefined territory. Colonialism inverts this condition, so that national sovereignty is instead claimed by another country. Although the colonial arrangement affords the colonists rights—from management of their government to oversight over economics and social affairs—the relationship itself, between the ruling power and the weaker indigenous population, is ultimately unequal.

Modern colonialism dates to the fifteenth century, when European states carved out lands in Asia, Africa, and the Americas. Over the ensuing centuries the reasons for these expeditions ranged from pure profit motives (driven by trade and the need to source cheap raw materials) to ostensibly more altruistic motives of spreading Christianity as well as European science and political systems. Whatever the motives behind them, the colonial pursuits of Spain, France, and Britain spanned some five centuries, altering political maps forever.

The neocolonialist charges that Secretary Clinton was presumably leveling at China were predicated on the idea that, as China continues to expand its resource-extracting operations in poorer countries, this unequal relationship between subjugator and subjugated is being recreated, and unsurprisingly, the American secretary of state was not a lone voice in the wilderness. Many other, primarily European and American, voices have been accusing China of enacting, in the most underhanded way, a strategy to assume sovereignty of countries across the world, including some of the most politically underdeveloped and economically (albeit resource-rich) poor economies, particularly many in Africa. Yet the fact is that the Chinese way to date has shown none of the trappings of European colonialism such as religious conversion, use of military force, or handpicking the local political leadership. What is more, the Chinese and, more important, many of the host countries presumably being "neo-colonized" see things much differently from these often-Western skeptics.

Simply going by the basic definition of colonialism, China is not going down this path. China's modern-day interests are largely transparent and driven by its dogged and narrow motive to establish commercial relationships. It is pretty clear that China's ambition is not for dominion over a sovereign state but rather over resources. Its foray—one largely limited to commodities, at least for now—is a mode of operation that flies in the face of literal claims of neocolonialism. In fact, China appears wholly *disinterested* in assuming sovereign responsibility and particularly in shaping the social and political infrastructure of host nations, and it has made repeated public proclamations to that effect.

If anything, China might justifiably be criticized for being too disinterested in the social and political constructs in many resource-rich countries. Although the Chinese have generally eschewed aggressive pursuit of political control, they have, in a sense, been seen to flout labor laws while disregarding environmental concerns and showing little interest in the politics of its host nations other than those that directly affect resource procurement. True, such a laissez faire approach will have a measurable impact on the societies within which China operates, but it's closer to anticolonialism than neocolonialism.

A Labor Contract

In the rolling hills northwest of Florence sits the little-known Italian town of Prato. Prato's population is estimated at around 185,000 inhabitants, of which 11,000 are officially registered as Chinese. Unofficially, however, sources count as many as 36,000 Chinese residents—roughly 20 percent of Prato's population. There are also roughly three thousand companies associated with these Chinese settlers, the combination of which has become a source of growing consternation to locals, particularly as the immigrant population grows.

Deploying Chinese labor throughout the world is a central part of China's resource strategy. Large numbers of Chinese workers often follow the global flow of Chinese capital. In Turkey, for example, police capture, imprison, and deport nearly sixty thousand illegal workers each year, as many as a third of which are Chinese. A 2006 article in the *Economist* further illustrates the reach and growth of the Chinese diaspora:

> In his office in Lusaka, [Zambia,] Xu Jianxue sits between a portrait of Mao Zedong and a Chinese calendar. His civil-engineering and construction business has been doing well and, with the help of his four brothers, he has also invested in a coal mine. He is bullish about doing business in Zambia: "It is a virgin territory," he says, with few products made locally and little competition. He is now thinking of expanding into Angola and Congo next door. When he came in 1991, only 300 Chinese lived in Zambia. Now he guesses there are 3,000.

Three thousand Chinese, that is, of a total domestic population of around thirteen million—not an invading labor army, but nevertheless a notable number that is on the rise.

The scale of China's international labor deployment isn't just about extracting as many resources as possible in the shortest possible time; the deployment also serves internal Chinese ends. Overseas postings bring down the nation's domestic unemployment rate, thereby relieving its own labor pressures and reducing the risk of domestic unrest, even perhaps revolution. Despite the fact that China's growing labor diaspora is a worldwide phenomenon, the brunt of complaints about these hiring practices originates in Africa.

Not surprisingly, as the number of foreign laborers grows, grievances also spread, including accusations that Chinese companies do not hire locally, preferring instead to hire (and import) their own workers. The veracity of these claims, however, varies from country to country. For example, in Zambia roughly fifteen local workers have been hired for every Chinese, whereas in Angola no more than one local is hired for every Chinese employee. The latter ratio is probably a reflection of the relative lack of skilled Angolan workers, a country that is emerging from many decades of civil war. Similar worker ratios can be found in other African countries that have also experienced recent political violence and instability: in Sudan (three Sudanese for every one Chinese worker), Mozambique (two to one), and Sierra Leone (nearly six to one).

As Table 8.1 suggests, the project at hand also plays a role in determining the ratio of Chinese-to-local workers. Chinese investments linked to projects that demand highly skilled staff—engineers and more technical workers—favor imported workers, especially in those African nations with a poor educational infrastructure. But projects with a heavy demand for manual labor—such as the Tanzanian village water system or Zambia's Collum Coal Mine—are by and large locally staffed. Ultimately, the ratio of local hires to Chinese workers across a sample of African countries is decidedly skewed, but in favor of homegrown talent.

The Question of Character

Quite apart from the sheer numbers of Chinese arriving at the shores and in towns around the world is the issue of these workers' character. Claims that many millions of Chinese workers are prisoners on work-release programs are widely circulated both inside and outside of Africa. These indentured laborers reportedly face a

Table 8.1. Fact, not fiction: Chinese labor in Africa

Year	Country	Project	No. of locals hired	No. of Chinese hired	Worker ratio locals: Chinese	Source
1983	Sierra Leone	Goma Hydropower Dam	600	105	5.71:1	Brautigam, Chinese Aid and African Development
1998	Sudan	Oil Pipeline	45	15	3:1	Human Rights Watch, November 2003
2007	Tanzania	Village Water System	500	50	10:1	Interview, Pascal Hamuli, January 2008
2007	Zambia	China National Overseas Engineering Corporation Project	n.a.	n.a.	15:1	The UK Guardian, February 2007
2008	Ghana	Bui Dam	560*	110	5.09:1	Labour Institute and Policy Institute, Ghana, May 2009
2010	Mozambique	Stadium	1000	500	2:1	The Africa Report
2010	Angola	Stadium	250	700	0.36:1	The Africa Report
2010	Angola	Benguela Railway	300	300	1:1	The Railway Gazette, April 2010
2010	Congo Brazzaville	Imboulou Dam	2000	400	5:1	Reuters Africa, January 2010
2010	Zambia	Collum Coal Mine	855	62	13.79:1	New York Times, November, 2010
On-going	Angola	19 Infrastructure Projects			1.17:1	Ministry of Finance, Angola

*Peak workforce was expected to be 2,600 Ghanaians and 400 Chinese.

Source: Deborah Brautigam, China in Africa: The Real Story: Chinese Workers in Africa, http://www.chinaafricarealstory.com/.

choice between remaining imprisoned in China or working off their time in some faraway mine shaft.

In July 2010 one such accusation of Chinese convict labor being used overseas gained a lot of airtime. An opinion piece written by Dr. Brahma Chellaney, a security analyst based at New Delhi's Centre for Policy Research, claimed that China was engaged in "the forced dispatch of prisoners to work on overseas infrastructure projects," that Sri Lanka had "thousands of Chinese convicts" working on infrastructure projects, and that convicts from China were also building four thousand houses as part of China's tsunami reconstruction aid project in the Maldives. Yet despite scant evidence—Dr. Chellaney provided no sources, evidence, or specifics to support his claim—his article was published in numerous international news outlets, including the *Washington Times*, the *Sri Lanka Guardian*, the *Japan Times*, Canada's *Globe* and *Mail*, and the website of the UK's *Guardian* newspaper.

But it's not just lone claims from individuals that are worrisome; around the world politicians—primarily when they are in the opposition and not the incumbent government—have made similar unfounded yet very serious claims. In June 2010, for instance, opposition politicians in Sri Lanka claimed that twenty-five thousand Chinese prisoners were working in the country. *Der Spiegel*, the German newspaper, cited a claim by Michael Sata, then an opposition leader in Zambia and subsequently elected president in September 2011, that eighty thousand "former prisoners" from China were working in the country. Proven or not (and often the latter is the case), these claims play easily into host-country fears.

There are fears that, because Chinese workers are known the world over for their productivity, instead of hiring a local for what should be a reasonably well-paying job, China's operations will theoretically bring in almost zero-cost, basically indentured labor. Adding to the furor, the presence of Chinese workers, prisoners or otherwise, is a particularly sensitive issue in poor countries that already face large youth unemployment rates. A 2010 International Labor Organization Report estimates global youth unemployment (those between eighteen and twenty-five years of age) at around eighty million. Because some of the world's most resource-rich and land-fertile countries have populations skewed to the young, with at least 50 percent of the population under the age of twenty-four years old, the pressure for creating jobs for locals is extremely high.

According to official statistics from the Ministry of Commerce since the late 1970s, China has sent around five million people to work abroad. Thus, claims that prisoners are among this labor pool are incredibly damaging. It is unsurprising, therefore, that claims surrounding the use of Chinese convict labor elicited a strong response from the Chinese government.

On August 10, 2010, an article in the Chinese newspaper *People's Daily* dismissed as groundless foreign media reports that China was sending prisoners to work on overseas projects in order to relieve the pressure of overcrowded domestic prisons. The article went on to note that regulations required that China's foreign contracted projects, enterprises engaged in foreign contracted projects, and related labor cooperation acquire relevant qualifications and assign employees who are technically qualified and have no misconduct record or criminal record to work overseas.

In specifically addressing many of the negative claims highlighted above, a Chinese official from the Commerce Ministry also argued that "the reports of China sending prisoners to work overseas are sheer nonsense and out of ulterior motives," and he appealed to the relevant media groups to "respect the facts and take rapid measures to correct their inaccurate reports." At the time of this writing it was not obvious that any one of the media agencies that had helped spread the story had, in the face of the China's strenuous denial, responded, retracted, or recanted.

Perception Is Reality

Beyond claims of Chinese favoritism and jail emptying, newspaper reports and articles such as the *Human Rights Watch 2011* publication "You'll Be Fired If You Refuse: Labor Abuses in Zambia's Chinese State-Owned Copper Mines" accuse the Chinese operations of unhealthy and dangerous work conditions, including poor ventilation, inadequate protective equipment, and excessive work hours.

These claims are worth investigating.

If nothing else, because there are legitimate questions about the way workers are treated *in* China, the labor hurdles to clear outside of China could be lower. That said, although the charges abound, the evidence is much more sketchy. And the reporting on this subject has exhibited a predilection for too much fiction and not enough fact. Part of the problem, as the *Economist* intimates, may simply boil down to misperceptions: "China is also often accused of bringing prison labor to Africa—locals assume the highly disciplined Chinese workers in identical boiler suits they see toiling day and night must be doing so under duress." In a camera-ready, mobile phone world, you'd think it would be difficult to hide (and easy to document) such transgressions, but in reality real evidence is scant.

As a result of the lack of nuance in this and other noted criticisms of China's actions, a strange schism has developed between mostly Western foreigners and reporters, who seem to prefer to paint China's incursions as unanimously bad, and the presumed victims of this abuse, the locals who often view Chinese presence in generally positive terms. Consider some evidence.

The 2007 Pew Report "Global Unease with Major World Powers" surveyed around the world to see which nations were most and least worried about China's growing economy. The number-one most-worried nation was Italy, where 65 percent concurred that this was a "bad thing." Second place went to France (64 percent) and fifth place to Germany (55 percent). (South Korea and the Czech Republic claimed the number-three and -four spots.) Among nations that considered China's growing economy a "good thing," the top three were all African: in order, Ivory Coast (96 percent), Mali (93 percent), and Kenya (91 percent), with Malaysia in the fourth slot.

When the Pew surveyors asked about China's growing military power, the results were similar. France (84 percent), the Czech

Republic (83 percent), and Germany (77 percent) were among the top-five nations who considered this a "bad thing." (Understandably, South Korea led the negative voting with 89 percent). On the opposite side the top-three "good thing" nations were a slight shuffle of the same African pro-Chinese triad: Ivory Coast (87 percent), Kenya (69 percent), and Mali (67 percent).

As for the United States, 68 percent of respondents viewed China's rising military power negatively and only 15 percent positively. On the rising economy question, the polling was just about even: 45 percent of Americans surveyed said China's growing economy was bad, and 41 percent viewed it as good. Asked specifically if China's economic impact was a "bad thing for your country," an identical 45 percent of Americans replied in the affirmative. In France and Germany that number was significantly higher: 55 percent in Germany and 64 percent in France.

Such polling data, of course, doesn't offer proof-positive that Western criticism of China's presence in Africa is overblown or that China's government-orchestrated defense against such charges is 100 percent accurate. But the data does strongly suggest that the closer to the ground you get in Africa, the better China's participation is viewed.

Balancing the sometime-valid charges regarding Chinese labor abuses with the positive elements of the investment has created a fragile situation for African policymakers. Not least because even a thorough search for data and proof does not yield hard evidence. By and large even the most heretical African politicians err on the side of the Chinese—whose investments are tangible and can help with poverty reduction and economic growth—while ignoring what many see as the ranting of foreigners. (The latter point perhaps reflecting the sour grapes of having missed the opportunity to engage with Africans on business terms rather than aid-based terms laced with pity.)

To be sure, claims that China's influence on African labor conditions is almost all negative can't be dismissed out of hand. Foreign powers have a long history of abusing Africa's workforce, even subjugating it. But critics of Chinese labor practices struggle to show evidence of a pervasive pattern or catalogues of deliberate actions with malicious intent by China to undermine and run roughshod over its hosts; certainly it is the case that if they have the hard proof, it has not been widely shown and forthcoming. The survey results cited above (and more data from the same survey to be presented below) argue, in fact, in the opposite direction. Remember too that China is happy to invest substantial cash in countries where the labor, environmental, and political strictures are more clearly defined; the Chinese do invest across Europe and the United States. Suggesting that China's actions or inactions are largely guided by the hosts' rules.

And what of the environment? China's harshest critics charge that its resource campaign will leave degraded and spoiled land, polluted waters, and depleted mines. They question the quality of the lasting "benefit" to the host nations—roads, bridges, buildings—accusing the Chinese of erecting faulty structures with inferior materials, again damaging the environment.

Finally, on the political front China is regularly chided for choosing to fete and court some of the world's best-known despots. Although China has certainly been willing to deal with undemocratic regimes that have at times violently suppressed free political expression, Western critics tend to avoid mention of the less-than-savory politicians with whom their own countries have done business. There is, in fact, little to distinguish the democratic standing of China's business partners from those of, say, the United States, which trades with Angola, Venezuela, and Saudi Arabia, among others. This is not to say that such actions are justifiable but instead to point out that engagement with regimes with more murky reputations (whether you are China or the United States) seems to be a necessary evil.

Shelf Life of the Strategy

Centuries ago, when European countries colonized the world, they made a fatal mistake: they did not take into account the locals' views and thus never made colonialism worth their hosts' while. In time this contributed to the demise of their empires. The Chinese have apparently learned from this experience, choosing instead to give their hosts exactly what they want—money, roads, railways—for access to their minerals, land, and so on: a win for all involved.

It might not always be this way. China might eventually have visions of colonial grandeur. In fact, history books are full of examples of colonial powers that jettisoned the soft approach for the hard— bullets, say, instead of Bibles. But with China's population approaching 1.5 billion—a billion of which still live in poverty—it makes sense to park any such ambitions for the foreseeable future. And this is largely what China has done. The country's strategy departs from the bygone colonial model in that the colonial link—and perhaps, ultimately, its demise—was based on propping up and establishing an unequal relationship between the conquering power and the conquered indigenous population.

To say that China's incursion is borne of any particular love—or hate—of other races or populations is to miss its unwavering focus on its economic motivation. In fact, China is apathetic or agnostic at best in regard to anything other than its resource crusade. Its sortie can be seen through the prism of the purest form of the rational economic investor. For China the rush for resources is a central part of an economic race from a revolution: the risk is that a revolution will erupt if China's billion indigent don't converge to the living standards of the roughly three hundred million in the middle class who already enjoy Western economic standards of life.

China is in Africa (and elsewhere) for the oil, the gold, the copper, and the land. To say that Africa is being recolonized—as is often proclaimed—or that the average African is not benefiting is just plain false. Of course, China's predilection for the African continent is not without its complications—any evolving relationship has challenges—but if the locals are to be believed, anti-China sentiments are largely exaggerated. On this point a further look at the survey results contained in the 2007 Pew Report is revealing. More specifically, three important points emerge from the Pew survey on how many Africans view the recent Chinese incursion to their shores.

First, favorable views of China and its investments in Africa outnumbered critical judgments by at least a two-to-one majority in virtually all of the ten countries surveyed: Ethiopia, Ivory Coast, Ghana, Kenya, Mali, Nigeria, Senegal, South Africa, Tanzania, and Uganda. As we saw earlier, respondents in the Ivory Coast, Mali, and Kenya overwhelmingly believe that China had been a positive influence in their countries, but they were far from alone. In Senegal as in Kenya, 81 percent view China in a good light. Three-quarters of those surveyed in Ghana and Nigeria hold an approving view, as do two-thirds of Ethiopians. In Uganda twice as many have a favorable view of China as hold an unfavorable one, 45 to 23 percent, respectively. In terms of trends, in just the preceding year, favorable attitudes toward China in Nigeria rose 16 percentage points, from 59 to 75 percent.

Second, the Pew survey found that in nearly all African countries surveyed, more people view China's influence positively than make the same assessment of US influence. Majorities in most African countries believe that China "exerts at least a fair amount of influence on their countries." In Ivory Coast, Mali, and Senegal, significantly more notice China's influence than America's: 79, 83, and 72 percent for China, versus 65, 66, and 54 percent for the United States, respectively. Even where countries view both Chinese and American influence as beneficial, China's involvement in Africa is viewed in a much more positive light than that of the United States. For example, 86 percent in Senegal say China's role in their country helps make things better, compared to America's 56 percent. A similar pattern is noted in Kenya, where 91 percent believe China's influence on their economy is good, versus America's 74 percent.

Third, across Africa China's influence is seen as growing faster than America's, and China is almost universally viewed as "having a more beneficial impact on African countries than does the United States." For instance, although the vast majority of Ethiopians see both China and America as having an effect on the way things are going in their country, China's influence is viewed as much more positive than America's. By a 61 percent to 33 percent margin, Ethiopians see China's influence as benefiting the country, whereas America's influence is viewed as more harmful than helpful by a 54 to 34 percent margin.

The margins are even more pronounced in Tanzania, where 78 percent believe Chinese influence to be a good thing (versus 13 percent who hold an unfavorable opinion), whereas 36 percent view America's influence as good, versus 52 percent as bad. Across much of Africa China's influence is already as noticeable as America's, and it is increasing at a much more perceptible pace than America's. In Senegal 79 percent see China's influence as growing, as opposed to America's 51 percent. Survey results are similar in Ethiopia, Ivory Coast, and Mali.

At the time of writing, five years have passed since this survey was taken, but there's reason to believe the numbers hold. The Chinese very visibly build roads, railways, schools, factories, and hospitals as a matter of practice, all (on balance) viewed as positive contributions of the Chinese engagement. Less tangible but important all the same is a commonly expressed benefit that, at best, the Chinese treat the local citizens in their host countries as peers, business partners, and, at worst, are disengaged about building anything more than business-based links.

Contrast this approach with the traditional aid-based stance, which has tended to foster an "us-versus-them" culture across many aspects of the engagement and thrives on portraying the recipients as helpless and not worth the effort of building long-term business relationships. Thankfully, this approach is changing, slowly, as Africa and other emerging regions are beginning to be seen as investment destinations, but the approach is also growing out of the fact that Western countries themselves are facing serious economic problems and can no longer rely on the traditional policy tools such as foreign aid if they are to have any semblance of standing in the emerging world.

Finally, the worst charges, that China is running its host countries into the ground, simply don't make sense when looked at from the perspective of a remarkable experiment charting the life cycles of diseases.

Life Imitating Molecular Biology

Gerald Edelman, the Nobel Prize winner, is said to have hung an attention-grabbing graph above his desk at the Rockefeller University in New York. The chart depicted the evolution, from inception to death, of some of the deadliest and most devastating diseases known to man. In plotting the associated mortality of different infections, from the bubonic plague to the French and British plagues (which cost France 66 percent and Britain 50 percent of their populations at the time) and up to the modern-day HIV-AIDS epidemic, a fascinating pattern emerges: in all cases the path of mortality rates follows a distinctly similar hump-shaped trajectory.

At the early stages, when the disease first emerges, the number of lives lost increases exponentially as the virus initially takes hold of a society. As the virus reaches its adolescence, it wreaks havoc as the number of concomitant deaths peaks—usually at an extraordinarily high number. Finally, in all cases, as the disease matures, the associated fatalities dramatically tail off. However, although the mortality rate declines, it never quite gets to zero.

The observed pattern reveals an interesting point. In the absence of medication threatening its existence, somehow the virus quickly learns that in order to survive, it must keep the host alive too. In other words, over its half-life a virus can move from ravaging its host to fighting for its host's survival so that it too may live. In an unyielding quest to survive, the virus mutates, evolves, and alters its complexion, discovering that it must adapt to changing conditions and coexist with its host.

Even if we compare resource-hungry China to a deadly disease—the most hyperbolic criticism imaginable—it is simply not in

China's interest to ruin a (host) country completely. Business investments need infrastructure—roads, ports, airports—and relatively
stable political environments to thrive. Yes, China's drive to acquire
resources is not without its challenges, but its leaders know as well
as viruses do that its hosts must survive—must remain successful
states—in order for the commodities supply to be met.

In fact, for most host countries the worst-case scenario is China's
departure. Were China to withdraw its investment capital from
mines, oil wells, farms, and infrastructure projects, the living standards of many millions of people would be severely and negatively
impacted, relegating them to poverty.

In the middle of the nineteenth century Britain's cotton was primarily supplied by the American South—King Cotton, the backbone
of the Southern economy. This trade suffered a huge setback during
the American Civil War, and Britain's imports plummeted, at which
point Britain (and France) turned to Egypt, investing heavily in cotton plantations. Thinking itself invincible, the Egyptian government
also took out substantial loans with European bankers, and the
Egyptian cotton trade flourished. However, when the American Civil
War came to an end, British and French traders abandoned the
Egyptian market, sending Egypt into a financial collapse that ended
in the country declaring itself bankrupt in 1882.

If China were to go the way of Britain and France and decide that
investing in a particular country for access to its resources was simply not worth it anymore, the host countries' vital cash flow would
be turned off abruptly, leaving its people in dire straits.

China Policing the Police

Because polls reveal that Africans' opinion of China is generally
positive and because the available evidence strongly suggests that
the Chinese are building roads and hospitals and providing much-
needed investment money to African nations while showing little

interest in controlling their host countries' political process, the questions regarding social issues must ultimately fall not on China but instead on the governments of the host nations themselves.

Broadly speaking, the government of an independent sovereign nation has three responsibilities. First, it needs to provide a suite of public goods—those goods that everyone benefits from, such as education, health care, national security, and infrastructure. Second, it should set up a broad policy framework that works to benefit and improve the livelihoods (economic and otherwise) of its entire population by setting in place positive incentives for citizens to innovate and work hard. Third, the country needs to regulate the way in which the society functions by enforcing the laws and policies that govern the country, including its social, and environmental, and political policies.

Yes, a resource suitor of China's wealth dimensions has many ways of swinging governments in its favor, but the ultimate responsibility for the sociological, economic, environmental landscapes must lie with the host country.

That said, it's hard to argue that a half-century of Western involvement in African affairs has done much to incentivize better government across the continent. Time and again the developed Western nations have chosen to treat the governments of poorer African nations with kid gloves, often giving them a free pass on egregious graft and theft of public resources while continuing to reward their government leaders with even more aid money despite worsening life expectancies, seemingly intractable illiteracy, and erratic economic growth. The villain is this system, not China. And only its *complete* overhaul—from one that rewards bad behavior into one that incentivizes and supports improvements in economic and living conditions—will turn the situation around. For the moment China would seem to be one of the forces actively working to improve Africa and the prospects of its people—not just Africa but also the livelihoods of hundreds of millions of people across the emerging world and beyond.

Taking No Prisoners

The late Massachusetts Institute of Technology economist Rudiger Dornbusch once opined that crises always come later than expected, but when they do show up, they are almost always bigger than expected. A burgeoning—and hardly hidden—crisis today revolves around China's massive push to acquire resources while other nations of the world and the international community at large have mostly sat on their hands. An honest appraisal of the future of China's commodity campaign strategy quickly raises questions about the future of Chinese interaction with its host governments as well as the international organizations: What happens if one country wants to restrict supply or expropriate its assets from China? Or if two or more countries collude against China and restrict its access to their resources? What happens when a poor country with no military prowess has vast mineral deposits that a country with military strength—and perhaps not enough resource to satiate its demand—wants?

The overlying issue here is figuring out the tipping point at which China does begin to throw its weight around and flex its military muscle. If only one country nationalizes an asset that China is accessing across many disparate countries, the impact on China's strategy could be relatively small, although it depends, of course, on the resource contribution of the country in question (e.g., one would feel the pinch if a large oil producer like Saudi Arabia decided to lock a nation out of its supply). But if two or more countries collude to deny China a particular asset, the picture becomes far more uncertain and precarious. Add a third or fourth country—a coordinated and collective action—and suddenly China's supposedly well-hedged diversified resource portfolio could be in trouble.

Thus far the Chinese global resource accumulation strategy has been executed without a need to resort to violent military attacks. China has seamlessly used soft power and its vast financial savings to court governments around the world and access global resources—making the commodity trade worthwhile to China's hosts without the need to draw on military action. Even when the Chinese oil company CNPC was faced with the nationalization of two oil blocks in Venezuela, China reacted mildly. CNPC remained in the country, and China kept providing the Venezuelan government with loans.

But for a large country with a rapidly growing military prowess, the exercise of soft power can often become less than charming once requests are refused.

History tells us that countries that are militarily stronger rarely resist—and will almost always resort to—the use of force to acquire access to needed natural resources from poorer economies with little military prowess; the Iraqi incursion by the United States and its allies is a recent example. Despite the penchant for aggression that China only rarely shows—think of the September 2010 fishing boat incident that caused a flare-up between China and Japan around the controversial, oil-rich Senkaku/Diaoyutai Islands—China's military strikes to secure resources are, for now, thankfully few. But nothing says this won't change in the future—if nothing else, under the euphemism of "protecting its investments."

What's the end game? China's stages may very well look something like this: rapid economic development, leading to accumulation of vast sums of capital and a persistent trade surplus, leading in turn to securing resources and raw materials, locking in global market access, ending with the establishment and ascension of China-based champions—the precursor to political and military power. Although China's leadership makes every effort to assure the world of their plans for a "peaceful rise," this is a daunting prospect not easily discounted. But the rest of the world—in particular, the developed West—to date has made almost no real or coordinated effort to confront this likely challenge.

It Takes a Crisis

The sad truth is that in democracies with regular election cycles, government officials rationally focus on "imminent dangers." Under the pressures of the ballot box, the urgent usurps the important. A more brutal way to put it is that governments tend not to care for future generations; these supposedly desirable models of government actually encourage political myopia.

When it comes to food, water, energy, and minerals, for example, there are clear signals today that these vital resources will not be enough to go around in the near future. As we witness the groundswell of the global population and as wealth and prosperity expand, global supply is struggling to keep up, but investment lags behind and nature's supply hits its limits. All things being equal, the situation will only get worse over time.

A policy attitude that waits for new resource supply to come online without supporting much investment to that end or hopes for depressed demand is folly. Yet despite all the evidence, the international community is doing relatively little to stem the tide. We'd rather not know. It would seem that we need a global crisis to spur us into action in order to avert a crisis—circuitous as this may seem.

Power outages, rolling blackouts, lack of heating and cooling, energy shortages, and worldwide food price demonstrations have done little to motivate serious action. Although such disruptions happen relatively rarely in more developed markets, these sorts of problems are commonplace elsewhere in the world. The demand pressures borne of rapid population increases (India's population is estimated to be increasing at one million people a month) and wealth increases, particularly across the emerging world, mean that the risks of shortages and disruptions to energy and water delivery will continue to be both crippling and chronic, not just in struggling emerging economies but also in developed countries. After all, we all draw from the same finite pool of global resources.

When the day of reckoning comes in the form of resource scarcity, as it most certainly will—sooner rather than later—who will be ready, stocked up with inventories, saved up for the rainy day? With precision, execution, and foresight, China is doing everything to be prepared for that fateful moment. But for the rest, without focus and concerted efforts many hundreds of millions of people will face famine, conflict, and worse. Perhaps this is exactly what the world needs to spur it into action: a commodity crisis by another name.

CHAPTER 9

A Harbinger
of Things to Come

T HE WORLD NEEDS to face up to hard facts: the commodities outlook is fundamentally bleak.

As we've seen, the prospect of an increasingly larger, wealthier
global population placing ever-greater demands on a limited global
supply of soft and hard commodities portends sky-high prices globally and, worse, could lead to conflict around the world as each nation, corporation, and person looks to satiate competing resource
needs.

While China continues to try and position itself to prosper in the
hard years ahead, the international community at large has yet to
fully prioritize the search for—much less implement—any mitigat-
ing factors that might offer escapes, diversions, or postponement
from a doomsday scenario of commodity wars. Yet though a search
for reprieves reveals little good news—and what positives can be located are predicated on assumptions that could quickly crumble—it
is worth taking a look.

The Shortage Is Food, Not Land

Each day around one billion people go hungry.

Amazingly, this figure has remained unchanged in the fifty years
from 1960, when the world counted three billion residents, to today,
when the global population numbers seven billion. Although the
hunger statistics are arguably getting better (on a proportional

basis), they are still enormous and unacceptable, particularly when so much untilled arable land exists around the world.

The dynamics of this situation are complex, but at the simplest level the issues surrounding global food insecurity and, ultimately, hunger come down to three subjects: food waste, misallocation of food, and policies that disincentivize food production. We take them up here one by one.

Waste

Americans waste at least US$75 billion in edible food each year, in part due to the 14 percent of food that the average American families toss. That's an amazing US$600 a year per household—a decent chunk out of an annual grocery bill—including meats, fruit, vegetables, and grain products that never make it to a plate. Research at the University of Arizona also indicates that 14 to 15 percent of US edible food is untouched or unopened, amounting to US$43 billion worth of discarded but edible food. But the larger picture, including industrial and commercial waste, is even worse. A study funded by the National Institute of Diabetes and Digestive and Kidney Diseases found that 40 percent of all the food produced in the United States is thrown out.

Not far behind, the UK wastes roughly 30 percent of its food. That amounts to about 6.7 million tons of purchased, edible food that is thrown out each year, or £10.2 billion worth per year (roughly US$15 billion). On an annual per household basis, that's between US$375 to US$600 of squandered food.

This waste in the richer countries has severe ramifications across the developing world, not the least of which is that the trashed food is enough to feed the world's hungry many times over. But the mechanics of this system are even more complex, as outlined at a meeting convened by the UK-based charity the Food Ethics Council. Government officials, food experts, and retail trade representatives described how buying food that is then often thrown away reduces overall global supply and pushes up the price of food, making it less affordable for poor and undernourished people in other parts of the world.

The costs associated with food waste also extend to the social, economic, and environmental spheres. In countries like the United States and the UK, for example, discarded food represents around 19 percent of the waste dumped in landfills, where it ends up rotting and producing methane, a noxious gas. In the UK producing and distributing edible food that goes uneaten accounts for eighteen metric tons of carbon dioxide. This, in turn, is responsible for as much as 5 percent of the UK's greenhouse emissions, the gases thought to contribute to global warming. To put this in context, if all the wasted food had not been produced, the carbon dioxide impact would be the equivalent of taking one in four cars off the UK's motorways and roads.

Meanwhile, the irrigation water used by farmers to grow wasted food is sufficient to meet the domestic water needs of over nine billion people. Quite clearly, addressing the enormous amount of waste offers a massive opportunity to gain a reprieve on the supply of food globally, with nearly incalculable positive environmental carry-on effects.

The developed world has made some progress in saving food from the garbage can and redirecting it to food shelters, but diverting edible food in small pockets locally is much cheaper and less logistically complicated compared with the mass delivery of excess production across the globe, as is sometimes done in emergency situations like drought or floods. Today there is nowhere near enough coordination to divert, say, the developed world's excess unprocessed grains to the areas of the world in need. There is, however, significant scope to ease the acuity of future food shortages by reallocating global food production.

Misallocation
The estimated one billion people on earth who go without food every day are almost perfectly offset by the one billion people

medically deemed to be obese, a disease attributable at least in part to overeating.

This shocking symmetry suggests that beyond the issue of waste, food is severely misallocated. But although reducing waste and more equitably allocating food are possibilities that quickly suggest themselves, they are also very expensive and, ultimately, should be unnecessary because many currently malnourished regions, like Africa, have plenty of tillable land sitting fallow. This unproductive land in the middle of a continent racked by hunger is, in turn, largely a result of a system of incentives and disincentives for food production.

We have already seen how each year many countries, including some of the world's leading industrialized economies, pursue aggressive subsidy and tariff programs that effectively lock out the agricultural produce emanating from the rest of the world. The US Farm Bill and the European Common Agricultural Policy each pump hundreds of billions of dollars toward artificially bolstering their farmers and their domestic agricultural sectors. By covering much of the cost of production at home, these subsidies price other countries out of their food market. Not only do these government policies discourage food production elsewhere; they actually encourage overproduction of food at home. The resulting trade distortions tend to disproportionately disadvantage the world's poorest agricultural producing countries, such as those in Africa and South America.

The United States and France are two of the worst offenders. Fearful of relying on other nations for their food in the event of a global war and keen to protect their agricultural markets and win the backing of their powerful farming lobbies, these countries have pursued trade restrictions, subsidy packages, and barriers to keep out foreign produce. In the United States alone the total annual amount of farm subsidies stands at around US$15 billion. The 2002 US Farm Security and Rural Investment Act has rewarded US farmers with nearly US$200 billion in subsidies in the subsequent ten years, US$70 billion more than previous programs and representing as much as an 80 percent increase in certain subsidies.

The US subsidy programs have the greatest effects on grain, including wheat, corn, sorghum, barley, rice, and oats, but they also include peanuts, tobacco, soybeans, cotton, sugar, and milk. Excess food production is often wasted or, in a nastily ironic twist, sent as food aid to regions where agricultural production has been decimated by the very government policies that have discouraged these poorer regions from growing crops.

In the case of sugar or milk the US government sets the minimum price floor for domestic production, whereas foreign producers have to pay extensive tariffs to bring their commodities into the US. Then, once foreign milk and sugar reach the shelves of American grocery stores, they are sold for (at least) the same prices as their American counterparts (usually the tariffs mean the foreign produce is priced higher than the subsidized domestic goods). Consequently, foreign producers are rendered useless to American consumers because they are not allowed to provide competitive prices. But the United States is far from the only nation distorting market pricing to support its domestic producers.

The members of the Organization of Economic Cooperation and Development spend almost US$300 billion on agricultural subsidies every year. Across Europe the Common Agricultural Policy (CAP)[1] represents around half the European Union's budget of 122 billion Euros (US$160 billion), with direct farm subsidies alone accounting for nearly 40 billion Euros (US$50 billion).

The effect of these policies on poor would-be commodity exporter nations includes huge hits to national treasuries. The charity Oxfam estimated that this trade regime of subsidies, price floors, and outright bans has deprived Ethiopia, Mozambique, and Malawi of potential export earnings of at least US$238 million since 2001. Oxfam estimated that Malawi could have significantly increased exports to the European Union in 2004 had market restrictions not deprived it of a potential US$32 million in foreign exchange earnings, equivalent to around half the country's public health care budget. Suppressing these industries also has a devastating effect on employment in the domestic farming sector.

For example, in 2003 US cotton subsidies to its few thousand farming families amounted to around US$4 billion. As a result of these huge subsidies, some six million rural households across the Atlantic Ocean in Central and West Africa were unable to compete in the huge US market, despite lower production costs. The potential trade blocked by these subsidies has serious negative effects on African nations. In Mali, for example, more than three million people, a third of its population, depend on cotton to survive; in Benin and Burkina Faso cotton accounts for almost half of the merchandise exports. Yet thanks to subsidies, Mali loses nearly 2 percent of GDP and 8 percent of export earnings, Benin loses almost 2 percent of its GDP and 9 percent of export earnings, and Burkina Faso loses 1 percent of GDP and 12 percent of export earnings.

In May 2003, discouraged by the market distortions that were squeezing them out of these large, wealthy markets, trade ministers from Benin, Burkina Faso, Chad, and Mali filed an official complaint against the United States and the EU for violating World Trade Organization (WTO) rules on cotton trade. The countries claimed that they lose some US$1 billion annually as a result of cotton subsidies, a substantial sum for countries whose entire Gross National Products (GNPs) average well below US$10 billion. Although cotton is not food, the effect of these US subsidies illustrates the devastating mechanics of such market distorting policies and the resultant dire living conditions for people all around the world.

Unfortunately the organization to which these nations turned, the WTO, is often powerless to fulfill its mandate of providing a legal and institutional framework for implementing trade agreements, settling cross-country trade disputes, and ensuring a level playing field for all. Individual countries can flout agreements and trade rules in favor of their national objectives with little recourse for the plaintiff, as the WTO is simply a forum to negotiate trade accords, without real enforcement power.[2]

Because there is no substantial penalty for doing so, other non-OECD countries have also supported their cotton industries, including China, with an estimated US$1.5 billion annually, as well as

Turkey, Brazil, Mexico, Egypt, and India, which put US$0.6 billion into their cotton sectors during 2001 and 2002. But the relative impotence of the WTO doesn't simply favor wealthier, more powerful nations who can afford large subsidies, nor does it simply end with market distortions that have negative effects on would-be exporter nations. In fact, this lack of enforcement power as well as the agency's poor coordination with other international bodies like the OECD contributes to the ill preparedness of the world when addressing commodity scarcity issues. After all, many of these organizations cater to the needs of their constituent member countries, with less consideration granted to the more global consequences that need to be addressed.

With its sizeable and growing population, China is very exposed to the potentially ferocious food imbalances that occur as available arable land supply declines. Yet ironically enough, the protectionism largely practiced by Western countries—and that international bodies have been unable to reform—actually helps China's resource agenda. Forced out of European and American markets, growers in Africa and other poorer countries with agricultural production capacity see large and hungry China as a very attractive market.

China's approach is building direct relationships across the world, creating at least two beneficial effects. First, Chinese investment—including but not limited to resources—helps create jobs and goes a long way in building self-sufficiency among the locals, who are then able to feed themselves. Second, by directly investing in farms and food production, China's investment opens the channels for trade in the foodstuffs that subsidy programs manage to block.

Structural

Of the billion people who go hungry every day, the highest concentration, around four hundred million, are in sub-Saharan Africa.

Africa also is the only region where famines have repeatedly occurred over the last thirty years, leaving the continent the only one in the world unable to feed itself. And yet despite these jarring facts, one-third of the remaining untilled arable land left on earth is also in Africa. This data suggests three things: Africa should be able to feed itself, Africa should be a net supplier of food to the rest of the world, and, finally, the situation we are dealing with is a fundamental, structural problem of demand not meeting supply.

Food production, at its most basic level, depends on the quality of physical infrastructure—roads, machinery, and irrigation tools—and on the legal enforceability of property rights and land titles. Many African nations blessed with arable land are also burdened by unreliable governments and ever-changing regimes, making for ineffective and sporadic enforcement of legal rights. No reasonable long-term investor is willing to invest in a place that lacks necessary infrastructure or enforceable property regimes. And it is for this very rational reason—the absence of both infrastructure and land rights—that many investors, both domestic and international, have traditionally been unwilling to invest in the African agricultural sector. Again, enter China, a nation willing to fill an investment vacuum with offers for infrastructure and the real prospects for sustainable economic development. China again satisfies its resource needs while appearing as a beacon in the midst of other nations' bleak economic environments.

An Energy Supply Reprieve in Shale

Fuel is another seemingly insatiable global hunger. For the foreseeable future fuel refers to fossil fuels like natural gas, coal, and oil.

With demand for petroleum on the rise and it being critical to economic growth, efforts to alter and improve the supply-demand imbalance of energy are just as important as possible remedies for the looming crises of food scarcity. Among other possibilities such as solar and wind electricity production, increased production of shale gas has been heralded as a potential game changer in the energy sector, a resource that could pull the world back from the yawning pit of undersupply into one of at least adequate supply.

Table 9.1. The shale gas revolution: The top-twelve hot spots

Country	Technically recoverable shale gas resources (tcf)	Proven natural gas reserves (tcf)
China	1275	107
United States	862	273
Argentina	774	13.4
Mexico	681	12
South Africa	485	n.a.
Australia	396	110
Canada	388	62
Libya	290	54.7
Algeria	231	159
Brazil	226	12.9
Poland	187	5.8
France	180	0.2

Source: Fereidun Fesharaki, "Asia Pacific Oil Market in a Global Context: Hot Topics," RS Platou 3rd Shipping & Offshore Conference on FACTS Global Energy, October 7, 2011, Singapore.

For the past twenty years the United States has been a net importer of oil. Yet by some projections shale may have the capacity to make the US energy independent over the next twenty years. If the country were unshackled from its external energy needs, the ramifications would be revolutionary. Economically, energy self-sufficiency would eliminate America's need for the more than ten million barrels per day of oil energy that it imports, money that could be utilized elsewhere. The United States would also no longer need to tolerate authoritarian regimes in order to gain access to their oil, leaving many despotic governments around the world more vulnerable and, thus, more accountable to the wishes of their domestic citizens. A shale revolution would also have significant ramifications for China and other countries with large recoverable shale resources.

As the above table shows, China, Brazil, and many other rapidly developing and energy-hungry economies are also those with enormous shale gas reserves. Shale could turn the global risks of energy deficiency into a tale of energy surfeit, a situation that would also offer a reprieve on global energy prices. Perhaps in anticipation of such an outcome, West Texas Intermediate (WTI), a closed oil market that has historically traded at a premium of roughly US$3 to Brent Crude (the internationally traded oil), was trading at a massive discount of around US$25 to Brent Crude by early 2011. Many oil and gas traders view this price inversion as a sign that a glut or oversupply in WTI has occurred.

As with many new technologies, panaceas, and potential economic saviors, much of the euphoria that surrounds shale and its prospects for transforming the energy sector is predicated on overly optimistic theoretical scenarios. As always, the story is much more complicated in practice.

The United States was already producing over seven hundred thousand barrels per day from shale as of the summer of 2011. US liquid production from shale (including liquefied petroleum gas, propane, and butane) is projected to rise to around two million barrels per day by 2015. In comparison, US crude production has dropped from six million barrels per day in 2003 to approximately five million barrels per day in 2009. Despite this growth, the size and scale of shale operations are enormous and expensive, making similar continued increase in production more uncertain.

Hydraulic fracturing, the process used to drill for shale gas, requires drilling more than five thousand feet below the earth's surface. These fracking and horizontal techniques also require huge amounts of water and can cause subsidence, an incident in which the earth moves downward, making oil harder to access. Infrastructure requirements are just as daunting. An average shale operation can demand more than two hundred frack tanks at a drilling site, eighty-seven thousand barrels of water to frack one oil well, and eighty to a hundred people working twenty-four hours a day for up to five days. Such demands on shale production mean a burnout rate of around two to three years on shale equipment, versus ten years for conventional oil machinery.

Furthermore, intricate technologies, available only in the United States, mean it is likely to be the only significant producer of shale energy for the foreseeable future. Yet the US shale resources are less than 8 percent of global resource. To further dampen enthusiasm, shale wells tend to have fast depletion rates and poor recoverability rates. The average shale well recoverable reserves hover around two to five billion cubic feet (bcf), versus conventional energy recoverability of around twenty to fifty bcf. In other words, many more shale wells are needed to generate the same amount of energy resource as one conventional oil well.

There are also very real concerns that the prospects of shale wells have been overstated. In August 2011 the US Geological Survey (USGS) revised its estimate of the recoverable shale gas in the Marcellus shale region, a sedimentary rock formation connecting eight states on the east coast of the United States,[3] downward from 410 trillion cubic feet to 84 trillion cubic feet, a remarkable drop of 80 percent. What is more, USGS estimates are intended to represent technically recoverable resources, not the amount of gas that is economically recoverable. So although shale resources may be available in sizeable quantities in theory, for practical purposes this source of energy may not be economically viable. Some market analysts have gone even further, casting serious doubt on the viability of the operations. In an August 2009 e-mail an analyst from IHS Drilling Data, an independent energy research company, wrote that "shale plays are just giant Ponzi schemes and the economics just do not work." Beyond economic concerns and wildly shifting estimates of reserves, the process used to extract the gas, fracking, is subject to significant pushback from environmental activists, who fear for pollutants and the contamination of water sources. Fracking is already banned in a number of countries, including France as of June 2011. US opinion polls also suggest that substantial doubt about the process exists among the American public. A May 2011 NY1/YNN-Marist Poll posed the question, "Hydraulic fracturing or hydrofracking is a process of splitting rocks underground to remove natural gas. From what you have read or heard, do you generally support or oppose hydrofracking?" Of around one thousand adults asked, 38 percent came out in support, 41 percent opposed fracking, and 21 percent were unsure.

Nuclear Promise

Nuclear power is an older, better-known energy resource that already operates in thirty countries around the world, providing 14 percent of the world's electricity. Yet even though nuclear offers some of the most cost-efficient energy production in the world, the industry has been fighting an uphill battle following the March 2011 Japan tsunami, which set off a deadly radiation leak at the Fukushima Nuclear Plant. Soon thereafter, both Germany and Switzerland announced that they would be phasing out nuclear power, a move that seems likely to place additional pressure on more traditional energy sources such as oil, at least in the short term. The shuttering, phase-out, or restricted expansion of nuclear power plants in other countries would almost certainly have similar effects.

China, though, seems hardly to have noticed the bad news for nuclear of recent years. In fact, its nuclear expansion plans are nothing short of awesome. The country plans to increase its nuclear power generation to around 200 GW by 2050, twice the amount currently produced by the United States. China is planning to construct twenty nuclear power plants and roll out thirty-six nuclear reactors over the next decade, a plan that, if accomplished, would be the fastest nuclear roll-out program in the world's history.

Of course, China faces major hurdles to meet its goals, including inadequate manpower, the absence of laws and regulations on nuclear safety, and challenges around plant design and risk of accidents; however, were the nation able execute its plans, China would catapult into the top-three largest producers of nuclear energy in the world. As an added incentive, the closer China comes to achiev-

Table 9.2. Who is using nuclear energy? The top-fifteen countries

Country	Megawatts	Nuclear share of electricity production
United States	101,229	20.2%
France	63,236	75.2%
Japan	47,348	28.9%
Russia	23,084	17.8%
Germany	20,339	26.1%
South Korea	18,716	31.1%
Ukraine	13,168	48.6%
Canada	12,679	14.8%
United Kingdom	10,962	17.9%
China	10,234	1.9%
Sweden	9,399	37.4%
Spain	7,448	17.5%
Belgium	5,943	51.7%
Taiwan	4,927	20.7%
India	4,780	2.9%

Source: Adapted from World Nuclear Association, "World Nuclear Power Reactors & Uranium Requirements," Nuclear Power Plant Information, International Atomic Energy Agency.

ing its goals, the more diversified its currently fossil fuel–intensive energy profile will become. Today, China relies on coal for 70 percent and oil for another 20 percent of its energy needs. But although pushing aggressively into nuclear power could relieve demand pressure on fossil fuels, China will have to meet an increased demand for uranium, a commodity that is a key component of nuclear production.

To that end China has forged ties and cooperation with countries like Kazakhstan, which produces roughly 30 percent of the world's uranium supply. In February 2011 Kazakhstan entered into numerous multibillion-dollar agreements with China, including a US$1.7 billion loan from China to Kazakhstan's national welfare fund, a US$5 billion loan for a petrochemical complex, and a US$5 billion energy infrastructure loan to help construct a high-speed railway line. In return China gains access to over fifty thousand tons of

Kazakh uranium. Faced with a burgeoning energy crisis, China once again offers a relatively poor but resource-rich country much-needed loans and infrastructure improvements in return for its resources.[4]

Demand: Here to Stay

The increasing risks of diminishing resources are driven by two sides: an insufficient *supply* of oil, grains, cotton, and other commodities and, perhaps even more starkly, a world of rapidly escalating *demand*.

Although both contribute to commodity scarcity, demand pressures also flip the script on the bleak story of dwindling global resources. Subsidies, protectionism, and the most disruptive supply-side market distortions tend to originate from the developed world, but the growth in demand mainly emanates from the developing world, where surging populations, urbanization, and rapid wealth increases are quickly driving appetites for both soft and hard commodities. Unfortunately, it's even harder to find some sort of relief from these burgeoning pressures.

Although there is some hope of increasing the global supply of commodities through new technologies or ending subsidies, there is very little hope that demand will slow. The population of the earth has more than doubled in the past fifty years and shows no signs of slowing down. India alone, as noted earlier, is growing at a million people a month, the equivalent of spawning a new Hong Kong and Singapore every year. The world in general is believed to be expanding by one hundred million people a year, a staggering number akin to adding a new United States to the global population every three years.

Even if the new rising middle classes of the emerging economies prove to be more prudent in their resource demands than the established middle classes of the developed world—and history offers few examples of voluntarily scaling back wants—the sheer number of new people on the planet demanding survival basics in the decades ahead is terrifying to contemplate.

A Message from the Energy Forecasts

Combined with this unprecedented population growth, virtually all forecasts point to stronger global economic growth into 2030, further increasing demand on the oil necessary to power homes and businesses. North America, even with all its structural economic challenges such as aging populations, debts, and deficits, is forecast to see its GDP soar from around US$14 trillion in 2005 to US$25 trillion in 2020. Over the same period Asia Pacific's GDP will go from US$10 trillion to almost US$30 trillion.

According to ExxonMobil, an estimated 2.8 percent per annum economic growth up to 2030 would increase demand for energy by about 55 percent between 2005 and 2030, with oil seeing a 40 percent rise in demand. In raw numbers this is an increase of around thirty-four million barrels a day, 45 percent of which will be consumed by China and India alone. Of course, it is hard to accurately predict economic expansion over a decade into the future, but even a relatively anemic global GDP growth rate of 2 percent would see oil demand rise to one hundred million barrels a day, roughly equivalent to supplying another economy the size of the United States with sufficient oil.

Energy Needs Increasing

Whatever the exact numbers, a huge part of this growth in energy demand will be fueled by China's rapid expansion. The International Energy Agency (IEA) calculates that by 2015 Chinese oil demand, currently around nine million barrels a day, will increase by some 70 percent compared to 2009 levels, contributing 42 percent to global oil demand growth. These figures seem epic, but they are actually relatively low when viewed through a common predictive modeling theory designed for growing economies like China's.

Generally speaking, oil demand has high-income elasticity but substantially lower price responsiveness. Higher income elasticity means that the quantity of energy demanded rises substantially in response to increases in per capita income. Lower price responsiveness refers to the trend in developing countries that energy demand abates more slowly as prices rise than it would in more developed, slower growing economies. In other words, people in developing countries tend to rapidly consume more energy as their incomes rise and they can afford it, whereas these same people and businesses don't slow their consumption very quickly when energy prices go up. Taken together, and given the economic growth trajectory (and rising per capita income) anticipated across China and the rest of the emerging world, these points suggest substantial rising demand pressure on energy, even as oil prices increase to reflect increasing scarcity. Although sobering, the relationships among population, economic growth, and demand on energy resources are relatively straightforward. Pollution, another major result of this energy-intensive growth, has a much more complex relationship to the dynamics of supply and demand.

A Problem with Pollution

For years Lake Tai, which borders the city of Wuxi near Shanghai, was covered in bright green algae sludge that thrived on the pollutants being dumped into the water by chemical factories. The situation became so horrific that the city had to cut off water supplies for days.

Today, the figures indicate that China's national water pollution is appalling: around 21 percent of its available surface water resources are considered unfit even for agriculture usage. Despite China's enthusiasm for erecting scores of rapidly growing cities, in 2005 nearly half of these urban areas lacked wastewater treatment facilities, leaving open and untreated water and sewage systems. In 2009 the International Energy Agency also estimated that China discharged roughly seven billion metric tons of carbon dioxide, a number that is expected to escalate to twelve billion metric tons by 2030. These environmental challenges go beyond simply inviting disease and reducing the quality of life for city dwellers.

In 2006 China spewed over twenty-two million tons of sulphur-dioxide into the atmosphere, a gas that contributes to acid rain, which harms plants, animals, and infrastructure. In some areas of China dense smog has blocked out the sun, preventing photosynthesis and driving down crop yields by as much as 20 percent. In other words, China's massive appetite for fossil fuel may not be stretching just its domestic production abilities in the critical energy sector; it also appears to be actually decreasing the supply capacities of another vital sector—agriculture. Simply put, a substantial scale-back on pollution could help improve the country's much-needed food output.

Focusing on the Urgent, Not the Important

Although some of the environmental effects of China's energy-intensive growth are horrific, the economic activity of every country contributes some sort of pollution, and the whole world is also subject to its negative effects. Emissions of noxious gases like mercury are released into the air or into oceans by China's factories but end up sullying the atmosphere thousands of miles across the Pacific on the US West Coast.

Economists would term the cost of this pollution a "negative externality" of Chinese consumption. But though China, with its lax or even nonexistent environmental regulations, invites the role of an environmental villain, its accusers in the United States and Europe have a history of their own to contend with; some might call it a double standard. In becoming the relatively wealthy economic powerhouses they are today, such developed nations relied on similar practically unregulated dirty growth over the past few centuries. During industrialization in England, for example, entire forests turned black from the soot of coal-burning factories. What is more, though China's growth may be dirtier on a national level, the country's enormous population uses substantially less energy and emits far less carbon dioxide per capita than, say, the United States.

In 2010 Edward L. Glaeser and Matthew E. Kahn found that in the cleanest US cities of San Diego and San Francisco, a standardized household emits around 26 tons of carbon dioxide per year—a home that would likely contain many of the creature comforts that draw heavily of energy such as washing machines, computers, televisions, stoves, air conditioners, heaters, and so forth; of course, this is at a much higher standard income of US$62,500. Chinese cities, albeit at a lower income level, emit much less. Shanghai's standardized household, for example, produces 1.8 tons of carbon dioxide, and Beijing's standardized household produces 4 tons. And a standardized household in Daqing, China's dirtiest city, emits only 20 percent of the carbon dioxide produced by one of America's greenest cities. China's relatively low living standards provide a reprieve for CO_2 emissions and other resource-related costs of higher standards of living. But as its population continues to grow apace, China's 1.3 billion–person population demands more washing machines, home entertainment systems, and the like, the challenges will become more difficult.

Although this discrepancy is largely the result of China's poorer population not being able to afford to consume as much as people do in Western nations, China's leadership does not hesitate to point it out. When confronted about its pollution record at the December 2009 Copenhagen Climate Summit, Chinese representatives rather mischievously conceded that they would not generate more resource-intensive pollution than the West.

This question of fairness—Should richer nations force polluters such as China to clean up its act, even at the cost of slowing the nation's growth and concomitant rising per capita income?—has made its way right to the top of the international environmental policy agenda set by international agencies such as the UN Environment Programme (UNEP).[5] There it might even get a hearing. International bodies and policymakers rightly devote time to individual issues such as population growth, environmental degradation, and economic imbalances—all tangentially linked to the fundamental question of resources. But the sad fact is that they continue to pay little more than cursory attention to the larger looming threat of actual resource constraints, as manifested by the absence of a global coordinated, explicit, and comprehensive approach to these concerns.

It is not that there's a critical absence of global agencies looking into "big-picture" global resource management, at least in theory. The World Bank, UN agencies such as the Food Agriculture Organisation, the World Food Program, the OECD, and the IEA, to name a few, all have skin in the game in one form or another. But too many are following their own numerous and fragmented agendas as well as catering to disparate clients and constituents. Meanwhile, China's global rush for resources is rearranging the world around them in myriad ways. *That* is where attention needs to be focused—not because China has gone rogue but because any thorough understanding of global resource supply and demand in the decades ahead has to begin with a thorough understanding of China's agenda.

CHAPTER 10

Clear and Present Danger

I N AN APRIL 1975 speech delivered on national radio, President François Tombalbaye of Chad, a landlocked country in Central Africa, made a plea for vigilance, cautioning the public that members of the army were plotting a coup d'état to overthrow his government. The reason for the expected coup, he went on to state, had to do with the Doba oil fields in the southern part of the country. This warning turned out to be Tombalbaye's last public address. On April 13, just days after his appeal, he was assassinated.

The simple fact is that the world faces unprecedented constraints in natural resources: from arable land, to water, to minerals, to energy—and oil in particular.

Persistent commodity shortfalls will limit global economic growth, consigning hundreds of millions of people to inescapable poverty. Moreover, resource imbalances—the prospect that demand for resources will significantly outweigh supply—will meaningfully reduce the living standards of households even in richer countries. As energy, land, water, and minerals become scarcer relative to demand, the prices of petrol at the pump, a loaf of bread, the rates on water, and manufactured goods from cell phones to computers and cars will inevitably rise. Such price increases will force commodity-related consumption either to decline or induce consumers to spend a greater proportion of their incomes on these goods.

But beyond these very justifiable economic concerns there is a much greater threat—that commodity shortfalls will wreak political instability, even war and assassination. Chadian president Tombalbaye might or might not have been murdered specifically to gain access to his nation's oil fields—he had made many enemies over other matters—but if resources were the cause of his undoing, Tombalbaye is at least in good historical company.

Past Is Prologue

Over the past two thousand years many of mankind's most brutal wars have been borne of clashes over resources. The Water Conflict Chronology List offers a sample: 203 water-related conflicts dating as far back as 3000 BC.[1] This extensive list catalogues times when water sources were attacked and contaminated as targets of military and terrorist objectives. It also accounts for incidences when water supplies (say, around irrigation access) were the root cause of development-related disputes.

But even in modern times the list of commodity-based conflicts is jarring. Since 1990 at least eighteen violent conflicts have been fueled by the exploitation of commodities, including ongoing struggles for land and/or water between India and Pakistan for the Kashmir area as well as petroleum clashes between Angola and Congo in the disputed Cabinda region. Such conflicts disrupt lives at the least; at the worst, they uproot households in the most humanly debasing way. But before delving further into the looming risk of greater resource-led conflict around the world, consider first how resource endowments themselves can be harmful to an economy.

The Curse of Resources

The well-known "Dutch disease" phenomenon was first observed in the natural gas sector in the Netherlands in the 1960s. According to the Dutch disease hypothesis, monetary windfalls that accompany natural resource discoveries adversely distort a country's currency by making it stronger and thus devastating the export sector and increasing domestic unemployment. Since Dutch disease was first observed, the pattern has been observed on numerous occasions and across many countries, including Russia (oil and natural gas), Chile (copper), Azerbaijan (oil), Australia (minerals), and Nigeria (oil) in the 1990s and 2000s, but also as far back as the sixteenth century in Spain around gold imports.

It works like this: say a country discovers oil. Suddenly there is an influx of cash from oil sales. (For ease of exposition we will express the cash windfall in US dollars.) The problem is that no one in the oil economy can spend dollars because the country's legal tender is in another currency (let's say pounds), and in the local market shopkeepers only take pounds. So in order to spend the oil-dollar windfall, those who have it must convert it to pounds.

The trouble is that at any given moment only so many free-floating pounds are circulating in the oil-based economy, so an inflow of cash makes domestic pounds relatively scarce when compared to the flush of dollars. In finance parlance this means that the pound appreciates or becomes much stronger—more expensive, reflecting its relative scarcity—when compared to the dollar. In other words, the value of the freely floating pounds rises as people try to off-load the more easily available oil dollars. A stronger pound means that goods made for export in the oil-rich country are much more expensive in the international market, making them uncompetitive—unless wages in that sector adjust downward. In the end, this chokes off the broader export sector of the oil economy and forces employees in the sector out of work.

Even if the domestic currency of the newly oil-exporting country is fixed and not freely floating—and so does not automatically adjust to the surfeit of US dollars sloshing in the economy—the detrimental effects of a resource windfall can be felt: the influx of oil revenues, for example, might increase domestic demand (as there is more cash available to spend from the windfall), which can lead to inflation. When spent on domestic goods, oil revenues also push up the price of other resources that are in limited supply—such as skilled workers—again making products more expensive and industries less competitive. In a nutshell, if they are not managed appropriately, resource windfalls can have adverse effects on overall competitiveness, wages, export-sector employment (usually in the form of a decline in the share of those in the manufacturing sector), and, ultimately, economic growth itself.

Resources as a Source of Conflict

Resources can and frequently do foment conflict, both within a state and between two or more states.

With regard to within-state resource conflict, unemployment and economic stagnation emanating from Dutch disease effects can lead to civil disobedience, strikes, and even political uprisings. The ongoing political volatility associated with Nigeria's oil-rich Niger Delta is one such example. Since the 1990s (in its recent incarnation) the country has been beset with tensions peppered with actual clashes and deaths—of the well-known activist Ken Saro-Wiwa, among others—between local aggrieved minority groups who felt exploited and (mainly) foreign oil corporations. Over the last decades this clash has spread from being an isolated conflict to one that has harmed the Nigerian economy as a whole and negatively impacted the safety and living environment of the local population.

More generally, domestic groups may engage in quasi-criminal activity to benefit from resources independent from the state; this also can be destabilizing to an economy. Siphoning off oil and selling it on the black market is often achieved through piracy and other activities of theft and violence committed by and on ships at sea. The value of natural resources increases the "prize" value of capturing the state and overthrowing an incumbent government through military action such as a coup d'état, so natural resource endowments are associated with greed-inspired rebellions and can

Table 10.1. Civil wars linked to resource wealth between 1990 and 2000

Country	Years of conflict	Resources
Afghanistan	1992–2001	gems, opium
Angola	1975–2002	oil, diamonds
Burma	1983–1995	timber, tin, gems, opium
Cambodia	1978–1997	timber, gems
Colombia	1984	oil, gold, coca
Congo Republic	1997	oil
Congo, Dem. Rep.	1996	copper, coltan, diamonds, gold, cobalt
Congo, Dem. Rep.	1997–1999	copper, coltan, diamonds, gold, cobalt
Indonesia (Aceh)	1976	natural gas
Liberia	1989–1996	timber, diamonds, iron, palm oil, cocoa, coffee, marijuana, rubber, gold
Peru	1982–1996	coca
Sierra Leone	1991–2000	diamonds
Sudan	1983	oil

Source: Michael. L. Ross, "How Do Natural Resources Influence Civil War?: Evidence from Thirteen Cases," *International Organization* 58, no. 1 (Winter 2004): 35–67.

lead to factional uprisings and undermine a country's political and economic stability through criminality.

In "How Do Natural Resources Influence Civil War?" Michael L. Ross presented thirteen case studies of civil wars linked to resource wealth between 1990 and 2000, as shown in Table 10.1.

Research around resource-centered conflicts *between* states is similarly rich. The common theme that emerges is that interstate conflicts are likely to occur when resource scarcity becomes severe—times of drought, for instance, or when water sources like lakes and rivers have been deliberately diverted or cordoned off, providing preferential access to a relatively small population. But there are other patterns to be gleaned as well.

According to Miriam Lowi, oil has greater interstate conflict-causing potential across the Middle East region than water does. One explanation for this difference is that the political and economic rents of oil (i.e., excess payments above what could be deemed normal levels) tend to be significantly higher than those garnered from water, for reasons discussed earlier: it's generally easier to transfer oil titles and transport and block access to oil than it is for water.

That said, oil's role as a motivating factor is sometimes not explicitly acknowledged. The Iraq conflict is one example: the risk of terrorist acts (and risk of weapons of mass destruction) and concerns around the subjugation of the Iraqi people were touted as the ostensible reason for the 2003 US-led ally intervention. Yet although often presented as an ideological dispute, the US war in Iraq can also be viewed as an attempt to control natural resources, especially in light of the fact that Iraq has nearly 9 percent of the world's proven oil reserves, one of the largest deposits in the world. (In this context the 2003 "mission accomplished" proclamation celebrated by US president Bush after the Iraqi incursion has less to do with the establishment of a fully fledged democratic state than with the fact that Iraq's oil spigots were presumably up and running once again.)

In its 2009 "From Conflict to Peacebuilding: The Role of Natural Resources and the Environment," the UN Environment Programme listed cross-country violent conflicts that have been fueled at least in some part by the exploitation of natural resources.

Predictions on how any one of these conflicts might play out are hard to make except to say that, for the most part, they show no signs of abating. In fact, in all likelihood the range of commodities that have spawned these conflicts around the globe will be the very triggers that exacerbate existing clashes and sets off numerous new ones around the world.

A Problem Hiding in Plain Sight

Because resource endowments are frequently at the center of conflict and civil unrest, it's entirely reasonable to ask if we can forecast

Table 10.2. Violent conflicts fueled by exploitation of natural resources

Years	War/Region	Participant 1	Participant 2	Other participants	Natural resources
1968	Senkaku / Diaoyutai Islands	Japan	China		Petroleum, Natural Gas
1988	South China Sea/ Spratly Islands	Japan	China	Vietnam	Oil, Gas
1975	Cabinda	Angola	Congo		Oil
1990s	Congo War	DRC, Chad, Namibia	Rwanda, Zimbabwe, Angola	Burundi, Uganda, Sudan	Minerals, Diamonds, Timber
1947	Kashmir	India	Pakistan		Water
2007	Palestine (Occupied Territories)	Israel	Palestine		Water
1948	Arab-Israeli Conflict	Israel	Arab League Tribes in Afghanistan, Pakistan		Water
2004	Baluchistan	Pakistan	Pakistan	Iran	Natural Gas
1991	Somali Civil War	Somalia	Other African Countries, the US, UK		Oil potentially
1980	Afghanistan	Afghanistan	US+Allies		Gems, Gold, Copper, Coal, Opium, Natural Gas
2001	Iraq	Iraq	US+Allies		Petroleum, Gas, Phosphates, Sulphur

Source: UNEP, 2009.

the specific places that are vulnerable to such conflict in the years ahead: What are the possible flashpoints of the future?

In a 2000 World Bank research piece Paul Collier and Anke Hoeffler provided some direction. They suggested that countries whose wealth is largely dependent on the exportation of primary commodities—a category that includes both agricultural produce and natural resources—are highly prone to civil violence.

Meanwhile, in "The New Geography of Conflict," Michael Klare argued that viewing the international system in terms of "unsettled resource deposits—contested oil and gas fields, shared water systems, embattled diamond mines—provides a guide to likely conflict zones in the twenty-first century."

Klare proposed mapping all major deposits of oil and natural gas lying in contested or unstable areas. These zones of potential trouble include the Persian Gulf (including Iran, Iraq, Kuwait, Saudi Arabia, Qatar, Bahrain, United Arab Emirates, and Oman), the Caspian Sea basin (bounded by Russia, Azerbaijan, Iran, Turkmenistan, and Kazakhstan), and the South China Sea, along with Algeria, Angola, Chad, Colombia, Indonesia, Nigeria, Sudan, and Venezuela—areas and states that together house about 80 percent of the world's known petroleum reserves.

Klare's map of contested resource zones would trace the pipelines and tanker routes used to carry oil and natural gas from their points of supply to markets in the West. Many of these routes pass through areas that are themselves subject to periodic violence. The energy supplies of the Caspian region are a case in point. Before reaching any semblance of a safe outlet to the sea, oil and natural gas supplies have to cross the seemingly eternally troubled Caucasus (encompassing Armenia, Azerbaijan, Georgia, and parts of southern Russia).

Klare's map would also show all major freshwater systems shared by two or more countries in arid or semiarid areas. These would include large river systems such as the Nile (shared by Egypt, Ethiopia, and Sudan, among others), the Jordan (shared by Israel, Jordan, Lebanon, and Syria), the Tigris and Euphrates (shared by

Iraq, Syria, and Turkey), the Indus (shared by Tibet, India, and Pakistan), and the Amu Darya (shared by Tajikistan, Turkmenistan, and Uzbekistan). Also included would be underground aquifers that similarly cross borders, such as the Mountain Aquifer lying beneath the West Bank and Israel.

Finally, Klare's map would highlight major concentrations of gems, minerals (including copper, which particularly affects China), and old-growth timber in the developing world. These precious assets include the diamond fields of Angola, the Democratic Republic of the Congo (DRC), and Sierra Leone; the emerald mines of Colombia; the copper and gold mines of the DRC, Indonesia, and Papua New Guinea; and the forests of Brazil, Cambodia, the DRC, Fiji, Liberia, Mexico, the Philippines, Brunei, Indonesia, and Malaysia.

Recent massive gas discoveries in the east coast of Africa—Mozambique, Tanzania, and Kenya—mean this region could emerge as a major gas producer.[2] But in a world of energy scarcity, the massive find also leaves the region vulnerable to incursions from militarily stronger actors as well as domestic turmoil as competing factions attempt to get their hands on the spoils. Already, without aggressive management, the risks and reports of piracy along the east African coastline could turn what is a promising multimillion-dollar gas play—one that could transform the region from indigence to middle income in a few short decades—into a hotbed of political turmoil and a flashpoint for clashes.

Beyond Klare's identified hotspots, water wars are already looming on the horizon. Propelled by water shortages, China is rerouting the Brahmaputra River to the Yellow River, leading to a face-off between India and China. The diversion is part of a larger Chinese hydroelectric project to dam the river, which raises concerns around both the quality and quantity of the water that would be available to other countries. (The Brahmaputra also enters Bangladesh.) Damming a river can degrade the quality of water available elsewhere, as many of the nutrients are depleted. Although Indian prime minister Manmohan Singh and Chinese premier Wen Jiabao issued a communiqué in December 2010 in which they pledged to enhance transborder river cooperation, such tensions are a prelude to other water-based theatres of conflict that are bound to erupt not just in this region but also elsewhere around the world.

The World Bank has identified eleven countries—Algeria, Egypt, Israel, Jordan, Libya, Morocco, Saudi Arabia, Syria, Tunisia, the United Arab Emirates, and Yemen—with annual per capita water supplies at or below 1,000 cubic meters, the minimum amount considered necessary for healthy human life. The average annual runoff in these areas in 1995 was 1,250 cubic meters per person, or just enough to satisfy basic human needs. Thus these countries could be among the hotspots for resource-based (water) conflict in years to come, particularly where water sources are shared and where one country siphons off water from what is ostensibly viewed as a water resource of another.

Although China does not feature strongly in the headlines of these raging and prospective conflicts, whether it is land, water, energy, or minerals, China's stealth (and not-so-stealth) global incursions will act as a catalyst for more global tensions around resource imbalances. Even more so, China's resource demand pressures will continue to force commodity prices higher. As the Dutch disease phenomenon suggests, those countries likely to be particularly impacted are the very ones that have the resources China sees as most essential for its economic growth.

Obviously all countries that are endowed with resources are not necessarily susceptible to conflict; other factors matter. Estimating the likelihood of a resource-based conflict must be placed in the context of the overall stability of the regions involved and the historical relations between different countries. Moreover, the success of oil-rich Norway in managing its windfall is further proof that conflict (domestic or cross-border) is not a foregone conclusion. (At the end of 2010 the money saved in the Norwegian sovereign wealth fund topped US$500 billion.) Still, logic and experience both teach that as global population pressures mount and natural resources become depleted, resource-rich countries will be as prone to clashes as resource-starved ones.

From Worst-Case to Best-Case Scenarios

The worst-case scenario for resource conflicts is not hard to imagine: death and destruction rivaling or perhaps surpassing that witnessed in the past world wars. A milder scenario involves maintaining the status quo. In this case the world population "muddles through," relying on the ebb and flow of global demand and supply dynamics. The assumption here is that although sometimes commodity imbalances will be big, most times the resource stresses will be manageable—say, as technology brings more supply on stream to satiate demand. In other words, resource scarcity concerns never actually become permanently biting.

There are more positive scenarios, more sanguine conclusions to the impending resource scarcity tale of gloom and doom. In particular, in the immediate term two arguments could defuse the pressure on commodities and force a more bearish sentiment (a view that prices will decline) around commodity prices and resource assets.

The first argument is the view that China has largely completed its infrastructure build-out. Having executed an aggressive infrastructure rollout over the last several decades, so this thinking goes, China no longer has a thirst for many minerals and metals (e.g., iron ore and steel) that are the inputs of infrastructure. To illustrate, consider that in 1985 China had virtually zero kilometers of highway. By 2007, just two decades later, it had over eighty thousand kilometers of freeway (compared to seventy-five thousand in the United States), by many accounts an ample amount of road network to support China's population. This being the case, except for substantially lower demand to maintain the existing road network, China's demand for resources—particularly iron and cement needed to build out a road system—could be on the decline. Although this argument may be compelling, the fact that China's urbanization plans will demand vast quantities of all sorts of metals and minerals to build infrastructure (pavements, piping, sewage and water systems) puts a massive dent in any credence to this argument. Moreover, even if it were true that China is nearly done with its road network expansion plans—hard to believe in itself, given the size and dispersion of its population—other commodities would be largely unaffected.

More generally, there is the question of how much further China's infrastructure rollout program has to run, including railways, ports, airports, and so forth. The precise answer is not known. Indeed, it is unlikely the Chinese authorities themselves know with any certainty, as their population is ever-evolving in size and location. But given China's ambitions to dramatically transform the lives of its massive population, the odds are that this train is still far from the station. What can be said for certain is that whether China continues to build out its infrastructure or begins to sit pat has enormous implications for the global metals and minerals markets because this underpins whether or not China is a buyer of global resources.

One more scenario offers a reprieve to severe resource scarcity and its horrendous consequences. This is the view that the Chinese economy is slowing, and slowing fast, and thus the economy will no longer demand world resources in substantial quantities. Whether China's slowdown is characterized as a soft, more manageable landing or a hard, dramatically negative economic contraction, the net effect on its demand for global commodities and, by extension, commodity prices, is bound to be the same: lower.

In the years after the 2008 financial crisis many of China's leading trading partners—the United States and Europe in particular—have suffered economic declines with concomitant drops in their domestic consumer demand. This, in turn, has had direct negative consequences on Chinese exports and, of necessity, the broader Chinese economy, including rising unemployment as workers in the

Chinese export industry lose their jobs. But during 2011 another story, which would prove equally bearish for global commodities, was unfolding in China.

It goes something like this: every five years since 1953 the Chinese government has outlined the main thrust of its economic development plans for the ensuing five-year period, as crafted by China's Communist Party.[3] As detailed in the introduction, the ruling Communist Party infuses government policies with the communist ethos and plays a central role in designing and implementing the reforms that govern China's economic development plans. As mentioned earlier, in its Twelfth Five-Year Plan for National Economic and Social Development of the People's Republic of China, released in October 2010, the government emphasized concerns regarding the country's rising inequality and sought to prioritize more equitable wealth distribution, improve social infrastructure and social safety nets, and increase domestic consumption.

To put the issue into context, China's consumption share of GDP (hovering around 35 percent versus, say, the United States, where it is closer to 70 percent) would need to rise substantially in order to help increase domestic demand and drive the economy. A view shared by many leading Chinese thinkers and commentators is that many Chinese households use large proportions of their income on education and health care. Thus, if the government wishes to spur domestic consumption, it needs to encourage Chinese households to spend more on durable or "white goods"—such as washing machines, computers, televisions—and less on education and health care. To that end, the government would subsidize households on public goods (like health care and education) to free up household income for greater consumption. So far, so good.

But where commodities are concerned, the tale runs into trouble—and grows bearish—if, as many believe, that rather than divert their incomes toward consuming more goods, Chinese households have in fact redirected vast sums of their wealth into the Chinese real estate and property market, chasing substantial returns. Although these investments worked well for some time, vulnerabilities in the trade have begun to show, as property prices appear inflated and countless buildings remain vacant. People who regularly follow the markets will be aware that one of the main concerns continuing to dog the Chinese economy is how and when the inflated Chinese property bubble will burst. Much like the US housing crisis that brought down the financial markets in 2008, the consequences of such a disruption would be devastating, and though the concerns of a Chinese property mishap are sometimes exaggerated, they are not misplaced.

What has this got to do with global commodity prices?

Well, some commodity price bears would argue that in order to avert a mammoth economic collapse—as the property bubble bursts, house prices collapse, leading to negative equity valuations and households' loss of the money they have invested—the Chinese government will have to make cash transfers to its population. These transfers would be used to reimburse households on lost wealth, prop up the domestic property market, and, perhaps most important, stave off a political uprising of the disaffected.

No one knows for sure how much Chinese household wealth is involved right now in the real estate market, especially as a lot of cash has been invested in real estate through a sizeable shadow banking system, which is not transparent. But the consequences of the property bubble bursting are likely to be enormous. If so, the Chinese government will have to draw on all its resources to meet a program for domestic household transfers, and this would have to include clawing back on its global resource campaign.

This eventuality—the withdrawal of hundreds of billions of foreign direct investment and loans from both the public and private global commodity markets—would be devastating not only for commodity prices but also for the numerous countries and hundreds of millions of people outside of China whose livelihoods depend on China's cash. Thus, perversely, a resource scarcity crisis could be averted because China, the world's largest buyer of resources, has an economic implosion. But this is not a strategy; it's a hope and a prayer—and also a pending global catastrophe of another sort.

A World Ill Prepared

Around the world governments actively police the commodity markets to keep prices in check. Policy tools are their way of circumventing and quashing any chance of severe global commodity shortages as well as price hikes. Indeed, without near-term government action, short-term commodity prices (before demand-supply imbalances correct themselves) would regularly skyrocket, perhaps enough that people take to the streets in protest. Understandably, then, governments step into the fray, occasionally even resorting to military force, to guarantee steady commodity flows and avert astronomical commodity price spikes.

The problem the world faces is that the sheer scale of the forecasted demand-supply imbalances are so big that the familiar or tried-and-tested interventions of individual governments will not be enough to avoid the wrath of global-resource scarcity and its consequences in a cost-effective way. A truly cohesive worldwide approach is the best way to stem the tide. But where is the global strategy to combat and counteract a global resource Armageddon? There is not one: the world is ill prepared.

Save China's remarkable, even Herculean efforts, there is little by way of a cohesive, coherent, or explicit effort to tackle the forthcoming challenges in the commodity space. Yes, numerous international organizations are involved in aspects of coming to grips with the resource challenge, but as we've seen, countries have mostly opted to address the risks of commodity imbalances unilaterally, at the national level (via subsidies, stockpiling, military incursions, etc.) rather than give the risks of resource scarcity the airing they deserve in a global arena.

True, focusing on national commodity pressures and priorities (via farm subsidies and the like) may appear rational in the short term even though these policy interventions distort the overall economy.[4] However, the longer-term costs of nation-state bias will most certainly be borne more broadly by countries across the globe because a nation-focused approach reinforces the schism between the commodity haves and have-nots, increases the risk of substantially higher global commodity prices, and becomes the crucible for future war.

As frequently noted by now in these pages, China seems to be the only country that is preparing for this eventuality in a sustainable way. But this leaves the important question of what happens when China ostensibly has access to all available resources and the rest of the world doesn't? Such a disequilibrium might seem hard to fathom, but even if China cannot physically hold every ounce of copper, own every barrel of oil, and lay claim on every water source and land tenement on earth, it has played one card well: it has made friends with its hosts. Not only has China gained admiration from other poor countries for the economic heights it has scaled in a short time; it has also made engaging with China worth their while, and this counts a great deal. It grants China priority access in virtually all corners of the globe, something that leaves it in good standing when the day of reckoning arrives and global commodity pressures reach fever pitch.

Forewarned Is Forearmed

Harvard psychologist Daniel Gilbert argued that threats must have four characteristics in order for us to sit up and take notice.

First, we must feel the threat to be deliberate, in that someone somewhere is deliberately trying to harm us. Second, we are spurred into action against threats that we regard as an attack on our moral framework and an affront to our honor code. Things like incest and pedophilia upset our moral compass, and in response we react in the most visceral and aggressive way. Third, we respond to threats that are imminent. The human brain is structured to care more about things occurring today than sometime in a hazy future. In other words, threats must feel imminent in order to elicit a response, arouse our reactive emotions, and galvanize us into action. Finally, humans react to threats that are instantaneous or happen quickly as opposed to ones that occur over a longer period of time. The former—a terror attack, for example—arouse emotions that urge action, whereas threats like widening income inequality or global warming, whose risks can become evident only over a longer period of time, do not immediately call us to action.

Dan Gilbert's work helps our understanding of why the resource challenges that the world faces do not get much of a global hearing. To the average citizen, particularly those living in richer economies and those remote from the places where resource-related stress and clashes are already occurring, the threat of resource scarcity simply does not feel real nor is it an affront to our moral compass, although environmentalists might argue otherwise. This being the case, what scope, if any, is there for a more cohesive global approach to facing the commodity future?

Stuck in a Rut

Why has the international community exhibited little but inertia in the face of one of the greatest threats facing the modern world? There are a number of possible explanations.

First, international institutions might feel powerless when up against national agendas. International organizations can hope at best only to provide a forum for discussion. In fact, given that they have members with vastly competing styles and agendas, convening is about all they really do. The actual agendas of these sessions will always be usurped by national priorities. Whether it's the WTO's trade rounds (Uruguay, 1986; Doha, 2001) or global climate conferences attempting to address environmental concerns (Kyoto, 1997; Copenhagen, 2009; Durban, 2011), efforts to set up rules and protocols by which all countries must abide tend to be scuppered by competing parochial concerns. In the end, the very discussions that could help all countries benefit in a more balanced way (rather than creating winners and losers) are themselves marred by chaos and an inability to garner any worldwide consensus.

These examples do not mean that some form of multinational consensus cannot be achieved around a resource agenda. They do, however, suggest that we ought to be less sanguine about the time it could take to achieve consensus. In other words, the sooner international policymakers rally around addressing the risks of resource scarcity in a meaningful, globally unified way, the sooner we can avert a doomsday scenario of painful commodity price hikes and increased global conflict.

The absence of a global agency focused solely on resource scarcity can also be explained by the fact that different countries value different commodities differently. These fractured preferences across countries further complicate the prospects for a unified global stance.

For instance, in India and other places across the emerging world, clean, reliable water is hard to access and thus valued with a high premium. It is not uncommon in these countries for water shedding to occur, in which residents have access to running tap water for only a short specified period of time each day. The notion that you could turn on a tap in a rich country and nothing would come out is hard to imagine, yet such an inconvenience is commonplace in many parts of the emerging world.

In a similar vein the ascribed value for gasoline is also influenced by a country's level of economic growth. In more developed economies such as the United States (where the per capita car ownership is amongst the highest in the world), people are generally more highly attuned to the price and, hence, the value of energy products (oil, gasoline) to power their vehicles. Of course, people in poorer economies use and appreciate petroleum products, but because a far smaller proportion of people in developing countries own cars or vehicles, often resorting to public or shared transportation (of course, bus tickets do reflect higher energy costs), the resource ranking is likely to be different. More specifically, on a relative scale oil is likely to be less important in poorer economies where most people make do without a private car but need water to survive. Conversely, few people in developed countries give access to water a second thought—its reliability and purity are assumed—but they are hyperfocused on the price of oil. Like most things, it boils down to politics. Water (its delivery or lack thereof) is a political sparring point in the emerging world, whereas oil is a political lightning rod in more developed economies.

It's a rare country that cares about all resources equally, but China has the makings of one. It is moving whole rivers to satiate its water demand, brokering deals around the world for land, stockpiling minerals, and rolling out reserve tanks that can hold mammoth volumes of oil. It will not always be this way, but as other countries climb the economic development ladder and their preferences and demands are felt, the pressures of resource scarcity are sure to be reinforced.

More generally, however—and regardless of the reason for global inaction on resource scarcity threats—what is true and undisputable is that there is an urgent need for one broad-based conversation about the commodity challenges that the world faces over the next decade.

A Way Forward

What might a global effort around resource scarcity look like? To answer this it is, *a priori*, critical to establish three things: the mission, the membership, and a metric to guide the definition of success.

With regards to the *mission* statement, a global conversation would be set up to define and actively manage competing interests as well as explore credible ways for countries to cooperate, share, and avert devastating resource crises, whether manifested as price shocks or violent clashes or, more likely, both. Defining the mission is a balancing act, as many emerging countries (and particularly China) have little appetite to make concessions on squeezing more out of the resources that are available globally, but those are the types of concessions that all countries will have to make. Remember, there is little room in practice to ask people across the emerging world to curb their desires for more Western-styled living standards, including plumbing, electricity, sewerage, higher quality food, and personal computers.

Linked to a mission statement would need to be some determination of the powers vested in any newly formed regulatory body. At a time when the world's appetite for large, stumbling bureaucracies is being challenged (the ongoing debacle surrounding the European Union and the threat to the Euro currency does not help), the need for a new global body is not a *fait accompli*. However, a code of conduct by which member countries abide, with applicable sanctions for those who breach the rules, is the only way that communal interests can supersede the ever-present national preferences.

Regarding *membership*: it is clear that countries have a penchant for imbuing resource challenges with their national purview. Thus, the more countries represented, the more national purviews will have to be set aside. Yet because the challenges that the world faces are universal, membership must be broad so as to capture a more comprehensive view of the situation and find more all-encompassing solutions. Strong emerging market representation is critical, not least because 88 percent of the world's population lives in the emerging world. China will have to play a prominent role, but the world needs economic leaders like the United States to get involved in a friendly, all-encompassing, collegial way. A peaceful world with accessible resources at reasonable prices is also in America's interest. China alone is not enough—even the Chinese authorities recognize this.

In a January 2011 *Financial Times* article entitled, "The World Should Not Fear a Growing China," China's vice-premier, Li Keqiang, reminded us,

> The progress China has made in development is tremendous, but it is still a developing country, facing grave challenges and has a long way to go before it can build a moderately prosperous society and achieve modernization. China's development will not be possible without the world—and world development needs China. We are

committed to work even more closely with other countries to create a bright future for all.

Finally, *success* needs to be defined: that is, what would be deemed success? It is altogether too simplistic to aspire for all resource-related crises to be averted. Although we might seek to meaningfully reduce the risk of resource-based clashes, it is nearly impossible to guarantee that skirmishes and clashes around commodities will never appear again. The population and resource pressures are too great to avoid some consequence. There is, however, no downside to trying.

The Real Villains: Self-Interest and Myopia

The current discourse around commodities—to the extent it even exists—is woefully inadequate. Any effort at meaningful resource debate almost inevitably ends up hamstrung by squabbling and finger pointing, with representatives from more developed countries using cheap (some might call it slanderous) sloganeering that cautions other countries against falling for China's charms. Faced with a potential commodities calamity, self-interest and myopia rule the day, especially in those regions and among those governments that should be leading the charge.

The United States' gridlocked political system is representative but hardly atypical. At a time when we should be learning to manage the whole earth's resource flow, the elected representatives in the world's most militarily powerful country can't even seem to manage states or cities or, for that matter, the nation's debt woes. Rather than make friends across a rapidly changing world, America has tended to (inadvertently) make foes. Or put another way, China looks to military options as a last resort, whereas the United States seems to consider them as a first port of call. (Diplomacy has not always been America's strong suit.) The resource crisis simmers on while American lawmakers rattle sabers, perhaps hoping the commodity explosion will come long after they are out of office. This is decidedly not leadership.

Ultimately the balance to be struck is managing the gridlock that has grown out of utterly self-involved parties advocating only for their narrow interests (China included) while garnering worldwide support and commitment for a global solution to the forthcoming global commodity-led collapse. Strike the balance, and the world's population might coexist in a harmonious, coproductive way; fail to do so, and catastrophic economic demise and global conflict are guaranteed.

Policy Choices Beyond a Unified Approach

What if attempts for a global, coordinated, unified approach to stem the resource tide *fail*? Such a scenario is not farfetched; whether it's Doha or Copenhagen, the international community has a patchy record of working together on big-agenda items. What other policy levers are available if countries need to go it alone? Realistically speaking, unless they are punitive, there is little scope for demand-side policies to put a serious dent in the resource challenge. Examples of this would be to levy onerous energy taxes to dissuade consumers from consuming oil.

The notion of asking consumers to scale back their consumption demands dramatically is a tall order, particularly when hundreds of millions of people across the emerging world are learning to aspire to the middle-class living standards of the West—replete with goods and services that absorb vast quantities of the earth's land, water, energy, and minerals each year. To the extent that consumers have already cut back, say in the name of environmental preservation, it has been nowhere near enough to meaningfully alter the core trajectory of global resource pressures.

Clearly, significantly more needs to be done. If demand-oriented solutions are not as promising as we would hope or as the world needs, solutions to the impending resource supply-demand imbal-

ances must largely fall to supply-side policies. Here are a few that
might resonate:

From Food Insecurity to Security

The 2009 report on Household Food Insecurity in the United States
published by the US Department of Agriculture's (USDA) Economic
Research Service revealed that one in six Americans lives in food
insecurity and/or hunger. That is more than fifty million Americans,
of which seventeen million are children. These numbers contribute
to the roughly one billion people who go hungry every day around
the world, across which fifteen million children die of hunger each
year. But the US data also serve as a reminder that the lack of food
security is not just the domain of the world's poorest countries.

Despite these harrowing statistics, the world could create twice
the food we produce if we were so minded and thus mount a serious
assault on the global hunger problem. Already, the world's leading
food companies and scientists have the knowledge and know-how
to increase crop yields and significantly alter the hunger equation.

So what is the problem?

Earlier chapters detailed how international policy hurt global
food production and skewed overproduction of food in some countries and underproduction elsewhere. But more than this, the global
food production debate has, to a large extent, been hijacked by technology skeptics, to deleterious effect. The many critics of genetically
modified foods, to cite one prominent instance, are so blinded by
their views that, in effect, they prefer to see people face the ravages
of food insecurity rather than have access to produce. Often, however, many of the claims made by antibiotechnology activists are
seen as baseless.

Take the claims made by activists that genetically modified (GM)
crops don't increase yields and actually have lower yields than non-
GM crops. In 2009 Monsanto released a line of soybeans in the
United States that has been shown conclusively in field trials to increase yields by between 7 to 11 percent. More specifically, Monsanto points to yield increases with herbicide-tolerant soybeans of

9 percent and 31 percent in Mexico and Romania, respectively, and average yield increases of 24 percent with insect resistant corn. Such evidence can at least partly explain why approximately 95 percent of the soybeans and 75 percent of the corn in the United States are GM. This is not to say that technology should get a free pass nor that technology is the panacea to the world's food challenges, but it is clearly a path that ought not be overlooked.

In *The Rational Optimist*, Matt Ridley opines on what it would take to feed nine billion people in 2050: at least a doubling of agricultural production driven by a substantial increase in fertilizer use in Africa; the adoption of drip irrigation in Asia and America (where water is directed to drip slowly and directly onto the roots of plants); the spread of double cropping to many tropical countries; the use of GM crops all across the world to improve yields; a further shift from feeding cattle with grain to feeding them with soybeans; a continuing relative expansion of fish, chicken, and pig farming at the expense of beef and sheep (chickens and fish convert grain into meat three times as efficiently as cattle; pigs are in between); and a great deal of trade—no small feat.

True, benefits of technology-based food production must be tempered by costs such as degradation to soil or medical problems arising from genetic mutations. But when we can reduce the suffering of hundreds of millions of people across the world facing hunger and starvation, we should unreservedly do this.

Water poses separate but related technological challenges.

"Water, water, everywhere, nor any drop to drink," Samuel Taylor Coleridge wrote in his famous *Rime of the Ancient Mariner*—unwittingly encapsulating both the global water challenge and the key to what must be at least part of the solution.

We saw in chapter 2 that although water covers approximately 71 percent of the earth's surface, 97 percent of it is too salty for productive use. If there were some way to convert saltwater into freshwater in large volumes and in a cost-effective way, we would be home free. Thankfully, through desalination the world has made some progress on this front, but like most solutions to challenges in resource space, these efforts have not been nearly enough to alter the worsening trend-line of the water scarcity story. To the extent that they exist, desalination efforts are still too localized at the national level (Saudi Arabia is a leader in this space), leaving the continuing risk that many countries will face savage water shortages in the not-distant future.

So where should future research be focused? Perhaps on making it possible to use salt water to clean our environments: flush our toilets, for example, and purge our sewage systems. Yes, this would require hyperexpensive dual-delivery systems for water, but saving freshwater for vital human uses (drinking and agriculture, most notably) might well prove a matter of life and death. The point is that if necessity is not the mother of invention in these cases, hundreds of millions of people could be doomed.

Energy

Imposing enormous taxes on fuel consumption could dampen demand, but the size of such tariffs would have to be substantial to impact the global supply-demand equilibrium meaningfully. If you are a politician, this is not the way to get elected. So what to do on this front?

There is a saying that "the easiest barrel of oil to find is the barrel of oil you save"—that is, rather than relying on newfound sources of energy, we ought to seek solutions for how best to utilize the energy we do have. This sort of utilization argument clearly faces push-back from the many vested interests in the energy sector—companies, corporations, and governments around the world—who earn hundreds of billions of dollars annually from exploring, finding, producing, and delivering oil. But energy-efficiency gains do hold promise to help relieve supply-demand pressure points. For instance, tax codes that nudge and reward consumers for saving energy (as well as penalizing those who don't) can create the sorts of incentives that deliver rapid action and marked changes in consumer choices.

These types of proclamations can often appear banal, but in practice, improvements in energy efficiencies are precisely where a number of sizeable and relatively easy wins could be had. It's not that people should necessarily stop driving their cars and other vehicles, but there is a great social value in consumers choosing fuel-efficient models (such as electric cars) over sports cars or two-ton trucks that guzzle immense amounts of gas.

A Treasure Trove of Metal

Environmental campaigners hold out hope for demand-based solutions that would see many more people resort to public and shared transportation rather than commuting thousands of miles per year in personal cars. Lower usage and demand for cars could substantially reduce the demand for metals and thus ease pressure on a critical resource point. Will that happen? Probably not, given the vast number of people moving into middle-class status. But metal recycling offers a way out.

Look again at the analysis of the extraordinary amount and value of metal contained in cell phones that we discussed in chapter 1. For just the United States, and for just one year, cell phones contained thirteen thousand metric tons of minerals like copper, gold, and palladium equivalent to fifty 747 jumbo jets. Just think of the impact to the mineral supply demand equation if we could recycle even a fraction of these. Yet estimates suggest that less than 1 percent of the hundreds of millions of cell phones that are thrown out or simply stuffed in a drawer (after a mere average eighteen months of use) are actually recycled. Quite clearly, the scope from recycling and thus recouping this single metal supply is enormous.

Until now our recommendations have focused on specific policies that could be implemented to redress specific supply-demand imbalances emerging in particular commodities—land and food, water, energy and minerals. But even on a more macro level, if leading countries redirected and reconstituted their public spending programs toward finding solutions to global resource challenges, the effects could be overwhelming.

Scaling Back on Military Spending

The total US military expenditure in 2010 was around US$700 billion (almost 5 percent of GDP), making it the largest spender by a long shot. By contrast, China, who holds second spot in GDP terms as well as military expenditure, spends around US$100 billion (around 2 percent of China's GDP).

The US purports to use its military armament to help keep the peace around the world. By policing the sea-lanes, directing its military muscle to help oust despots, and defusing political insurrections, the US underwrites the costs of maintaining some semblance of peace across the globe. This view is not without merit, and although many US involvements are colored by its nationalist agenda, many countries around the world turn to the US for guidance and seek military action. In recent times, for example, brewing tensions in the South China Sea and discomfort around China's growing military strength and regional dominance have led a number of Asian countries to ask the United States for more involvement in the Asian-Pacific region.

But what might actually happen if the United States were to cut back its military spending and instead redirect that money to R&D investments in pursuit of long-term solutions to the shortages in food, water, energy, and minerals facing the world?

It is not at all obvious that the world would descend into more or greater clashes than the world already witnesses each day. In fact, a compelling case can be made that were the United States *less* predisposed to military action, there might be fewer clashes in the world. Over time a by-product of redirecting American money toward global commodity solutions might well be that the United States would find itself engaged in fewer conflicts that have at least elements of resource supply-demand imbalance in their origins.

But there is another benefit. Any progress the United States would make in solving the global commodity scarcity issues—whether through direct government involvement or by encouraging private-sector initiatives—would permeate the globe and benefit the world as a whole. As the Pew polling we saw in chapter 8 suggests,

America needs to restore its status as a light to the world. What better way than this?

The trade-off the US society must grapple with is straightforward: Should America be a force for good—one that seeks to solve problems like resource scarcity afflicting the globe and enhance the well-being of people's lives and human existence around the world? Or does the United States wish to push for short-term solutions with nationalistic leanings that are increasingly untenable and will continue to lead to a world marred in conflicts that wreak death and destruction?

Heading into the Eye of the Storm

Many demographers believe that the proliferation in the world's population occurring at present is the continuation of an extraordinary trend that started about two centuries ago and has gathered momentum since the beginning of the twentieth century.

The bad news is that this trend of rapid and extensive growth is set to continue well into 2050, when forecasts put the size of the global population over nine billion. Based on the analysis presented in this book, the earth simply does not have adequate resources to support this population, particularly not at the living standard at which many hundreds of millions of people have grown accustomed.

The good news is that, when set in historical context, the ongoing explosion in the world's population can be viewed as a unique episode—unprecedented in history. And once the present trend has run its course, it is highly unlikely that any such expansion in population, in terms of the speed and magnitude, will ever occur again. The best guess from the United Nations is that the world population will start to decline in 2075 once it reaches 9.2 billion. In other words, the world population will not grow ad infinitum, and there likely will be a reprieve from commodity demand pressures. China itself risks getting old before getting rich, with some estimates suggesting that half of China's population will be fifty years old or older by 2050. This could put a damper on the demand of commodities, as the young (not the elderly) people usually drive consumption.

Here's the inescapable issue, though: such dramatic changes in composition are unlikely to occur for some time yet. This fact means that we find ourselves on earth at a unique time with the extraordinary challenge of managing and navigating the headwinds of commodity shortages that the world faces over the next two decades. At present we are ill prepared to contend with this eventuality, yet the challenges we face go beyond our living standards to the survival of the planet as we know it. This fight is about life or death.

List of Tables and Figures

Acknowledgments

I loved researching and writing this book.

I learned a lot about the workings of the commodity markets—most of it fascinating, parts of it frightening.

From concept to cover, I had the great privilege of meeting and spending time with representatives and actors from all the key spheres of the commodity industry:

- the government representatives that sell their sovereign commodity assets;
- the Chinese policymakers and international business people that buy resources from around the world;
- the hedge fund managers who trade resources everyday; and
- the miners, farmers and oil engineers that mine, grow, and extract the range of commodities that miraculously appear in our supermarkets and gas stations.

Through the writing process, I benefited from the kindness and unwavering support of a number of people.

Foremost is my best friend, Iris, who, as always, kept me laughing and sane, particularly during the rough patches. (I promise to get us each a psychiatrist if I decide to write another book.)

Others who had a hand in the making of the book are, in alphabetical order, Jeremy Adams, Pritish Behuria, Jeremy Brenner, Paula Cooper, Howard Means, Nathan Means, Roxana Mohammadian-Molina, Susana Moreira, Daniel Rosen, and Derek Scissors helped with data, insights, research and/or editorial work.

David Cherrett, Bill McCahill, Chris Rokos, Emmanuel (Manny) Roman, and Geordie Young each deserves a special mention for giving this book a detailed and critical look and for granting me numerous hours of discussion. Kevin Currey provided fantastic research support. I thank you all most sincerely. That said, all errors and fillips are my own.

My literary agent Andrew Wylie was indefatigable and indomitable, as was James Pullen and the rest of the team at the Wylie Agency. If only all aspects of my life ran as efficiently!

The invisible hand of any book is the editors. For me the champions, through thick and thin, were the team at Basic Books (the Perseus Books Group), in particular Tim Bartlett, and the Penguin team led by Will Goodlad, and latterly Tom Penn.

Finally, as always, the book is dedicated to my family in Zambia. I thank you for leading the way and reminding me that, even against the odds, anything is possible.

Notes

Introduction

1. Peru's 2010 per capita income was around US$9,000, versus around US$45,000 in the United States.

2. "China's Peaceful Rise: Speeches of Zheng Bijian 1997–2004," http://www.brookings.edu/fp/events/20050616bijianlunch.pdf.

3. In China, permissioning agencies are government-based organizations that control how corporations and people conduct business in the country. If a company, corporation, or individual wishes to conduct business in China, it must obtain a number of separate forms of consent from the government. For example, for the purposes of registration certification, it must obtain a "business license of enterprise legal person" with the State Administration for Industry and Commerce. The entity must also be granted approval from the police department to make a company seal and must acquire an organization code certificate from the Quality and Technology Supervision Bureau.

4. Similarly, at the onset of the bird flu in the mid-2000s China is thought to have slaughtered two million birds in a matter of days to avert its spread.

5. It is worth noting that there is some evidence that a large share of the oil Chinese companies produce overseas is actually not sent back to China. In fact, some Chinese oil firms play up Chinese fears of not having enough oil so that the companies can obtain cheap funding and greater government/political support for their international ventures.

Chapter 1

1. Of course when the staggering human population dynamics (size of the world population as well as rising wealth) is added to resource pressures of animals and plants, the draw on resources (certainly arable land and water) is even more severe.

2. GDP per capita statistics can be misleading. They mask the challenge of poverty reduction because the per capita income measure is impacted by population size, so even if two countries have the same income, the country with a larger population has a smaller per capita income measure and is thus poorer than the country with a smaller population.

3. Gini coefficients are used in economics to measure income inequality of a population. A value of 0 represents total equality and a value of 100 reflects total inequality. According to the "Distribution of Family Income—GINI Index," *The World Factbook*, https://www.cia.gov/library/publications/the-world-factbook/rankorder/2172rank.html, in October 2011 China's gini coefficient was 41.5 in 2007, as compared to the United States at 45.0 in the same year.

4. A substitution effect refers to changes in demand in the quality and quantity of goods accompanied with changes in income.

5. This is calculated as follows: a Boeing 747-400 jet that seats at least four hundred people has a zero-fuel weight—that is, the weight of the plane and all its contents less the weight of the fuel on board—of around 251,740 kilograms (or 555,000 pounds). This translates into approximately 251 metric tons. If the total weight of the metal in cell phones is around 13,000 metric tons (the 2004 estimate in Chapter 1), this roughly equates to around fifty jumbo jets.

6. China's commodity demands are massive. Every year it invests around US$116 per capita on capital investments in urban infrastructure.

Chapter 2

1. According to the FAO, arable land is "the land under temporary agricultural crops (multiple-cropped areas are counted only once), temporary meadows for mowing or pasture, land under market and kitchen gardens and land temporarily fallow (less than five years)" (FAO Statistics Division 2011).

2. The UN Food and Agricultural Organization (FAO) is mandated to "raise levels of nutrition, improve agricultural productivity, better the lives of rural populations and contribute to the growth of the world economy" and "achieving food security for all—to make sure people have regular access to enough high-quality food to lead active, healthy lives."

3. According to the FAO, total actual renewable water resources is the "sum of internal renewable water resources and external actual renewable

water resources. It corresponds to the maximum theoretical yearly amount of water actually available for a country at a given moment."

4. In fact, it was American scientists who made the crucial breakthrough of creating and controlling rain in a laboratory in 1946.

Chapter 3

1. The International Energy Agency (IEA) is an independent organization seeking to ensure reliable, affordable, and clean energy for its twenty-eight member countries and beyond. According to its website, http://www.iea.org/about/index.asp, the organization's four main areas of focus are (1) energy security: promoting diversity, efficiency, and flexibility within all energy sectors; (2) economic development: ensuring the stable supply of energy to IEA member countries and promoting free markets to foster economic growth and eliminate energy poverty; (3) environmental awareness: enhancing international knowledge of options for tackling climate change; and (4) engagement worldwide: working closely with nonmember countries, especially major producers and consumers, to find solutions to shared energy and environmental concerns.

2. The 2008 financial crisis has placed significant challenges on the energy sector. For instance, the decline in global GDP of around 1.7 percent in 2009 led to a forecast reduction in oil demand by 1.4 million barrels per day and an accompanying sharp collapse in oil prices. In the two years immediately after the crisis the price of oil fell by over 50 percent from the peaks in 2008, rendering many resource projects unprofitable and unsustainable. The financial crisis restricted the availability of equity and debt, thus causing the cost of capital to rise precipitously and set back investment and projects by as much as five years (as these became too expensive to finance). Worse still, during the financial crisis banks were forced to review the borrowing capacity of oil companies, and they began to use lower oil prices (US$40–50 per barrel) as a guide to model corporate cash flows and profitability. But as discussed earlier, US$50 is the threshold price for many oil producers to stay open for business. So the lower oil price assumptions (reflecting the worsening global economic conditions) lowered the borrowing capacity across oil companies. With no capital on offer, companies faced a liquidity squeeze that hurt their operations, often leaving them unable to service their debt obligations and, in some cases, leading them to outright default.

3. As opposed to coal, which is more equitable, as 42 percent of people control 50 percent of the resource.

4. Top-ten hard-coal producers (metric tons in hundred thousands):

China	2,971
United States	919
India	526
Australia	335
Indonesia	263
South Africa	247
Russia	229
Kazakhstan	96
Poland	78
Colombia	73

Source: Benjamin Sporton, World Coal Institute Presentation, Global Coal Dynamics, VI Columbia Minera, October 6, 2010.

5. More information on coal can be viewed at "Environmental Impacts of Coal Power: Water Use," Union of Concerned Scientists, http://www.ucsusa.org/clean_energy/coalvswind/co2b.html.

6. The US Energy Information Administration (EIA) is part of the US Department of Energy and is responsible for collating, analyzing, and distributing statistical information on the energy markets.

7. Schlumberger's Supply Gap Analysis further explained: take their 30 million barrels of daily oil output projected for 2030. Add to this the 2030 forecasted daily gas production of around 20 million BOE (much more discussion on gas as a source of energy to come later in the chapter) to get roughly 50 million BOE a day from these fossil fuels (oil and gas). Then add the projected additional capacity (say, from technology improvements) from projects coming on stream between 2008 and 2015. For this, the current estimates are gauged at a rate of around 5.5 million BOE a day each year along with capacity additions between 2016 and 2030 based on current rate of investment (an additional 80 million BOE a year) get us to around 130 million barrels of oil and gas production a day in total.

8. It is worth noting, however, that natural gas can be an important source of electricity when used in thermal plants.

9. More generally, the consequences of emerging economies (led by China and India), with around 5.4 billion people consuming around 35.2 million barrels of oil per day, converging to industrialized-country con-

sumption levels, with a 1.2 billion population and oil consumption patterns at 49.3 million barrels per day, are enormous.

10. There is increasing interest global demand for a class of seventeen minerals known as rare earths. These minerals have a range of uses, including as inputs into the manufacture of mobile phones, X-ray and MRI scanning systems, camera and telescope lenses, catalytic converters in cars, aircraft engines, computers and televisions. China is the predominant supplier of rare earth metals and according to the US Geological Survey, China produced 130,000 metric tons of rare-earth oxide in 2011, 97 percent of global production, and has 55 million metric tons in reserves, about 50 percent of global reserves. Further, China has imposed export quotas on rare earths, causing consternation with other economies such as the United States and leading the EU and the United States to file a complaint in March 2012 with the WTO about China's export quotas.

11. The Organization for Economic Cooperation and Development (OECD), comprised of thirty-four countries, is an advisory group that recommends policies to promote worldwide social and economic prosperity.

Chapter 4

1. The Chinese currency (renminbi or yuan) is managed and controlled by the Chinese central bank (equivalent to the US Federal Reserve). The currency is managed to float in a narrow margin determined with reference to a basket of world currencies. This currency has been a source of consternation for many of China's trading partners (especially the United States), who have accused China of keeping its currency artificially cheap relative to other currencies (such as the US dollar). This helps Chinese trade competitiveness, bolstering Chinas exports, and it disadvantages the US trade position, which ends up with a sizeable deficit, as the US imports a significant amount of Chinese goods.

2. Additionally, the International Energy Agency February 2011 information report entitled, "Overseas Investments by Chinese National Oil Companies: Assessing the Drivers and Impacts," provides detailed information on Chinese foreign oil and gas acquisition deals since 2002.

Chapter 5

1. Commodity price indices are weighted indices of selected commodity prices, which may be based on spot or futures prices. They are structured to

reflect a broad commodity asset class or a specific subset of commodities, such as energy or metals, and offer an opportunity for investors to get commodity exposures by investing in the various indices.

2. Of course, the price elasticity of a commodity (i.e., how the demand for the resource changes with the change in its price) also impacts commodity investment decisions.

3. Financial positions can yield positive carry on balance sheets (i.e., assets that produce sustained and positive cash flows) or negative carry on balance sheets, which produce no interim cash flows, or cash flows that do not cover the cost of borrowing.

4. In practice, one needs three variables to estimate the forward price of an asset (e.g., bonds). These are the spot or today's price of the asset, the risk-free rate, and the cost of carry (also known as the financing charge). The same is true for commodities, except in this case the cost of carry must be adjusted by the convenience yield in order to reflect the benefit of actually holding the physical commodity.

5. Short-selling or shorting is the act of selling securities or assets that have been borrowed from a third party, often a broker.

6. The reservation price is the maximum price a consumer will pay or the minimum price a producer will sell for.

Chapter 6

1. This story is an abridged version from a speech made by Deborah Brautigam at the China's Engagement with Africa Conference in Washington, DC, on July 28, 2010.

2. China's purchases of US treasury bonds would have pushed yields (or interest rates) down. One effect of this is to increase the value of long-date pension liabilities. If the value of pension assets remains constant, the net pension position (calculated as assets minus liabilities) worsens.

3. Countries that are part of a global economy could import inflation. Countries are affected by oil price movements even if domestic oil dynamics work.

4. OPEC's oil exports account for about 70 percent of the oil traded internationally and generates two-thirds of the world's oil reserves.

Chapter 7

1. In practice, the Chinese government population control decree restricts less than 40 percent of the population to having only one child. The

one-child policy applies to a minority of families, such as married, urban couples, whereas rural couples, ethnic minorities, and parents without any siblings are exempt from the law, thereby adding to population pressures and, ultimately, to resource pressures, as rising populations invariably contribute to rising commodity demand. See Guan Xiaofung, "Most People Free to Have More Child(ren)," *China Daily*, http://www2.chinadaily.com.cn/china/2007-07/11/content_5432238.htm.

2. A first-lien position means that, in the event that the loan is in default and the property is to be sold, the lender is in the first (or priority position) to benefit from any liquidation of the collateral that secures the loan.

3. According to the Norges Bank Investment Management (NBIM) website (http://www.nbim.no/en/About-us/Government-Pension-Fund-Global/), NBIM is accumulating wealth to aid government fiscal policy in case of a future fall in oil prices, a decline in Norway's oil availability, and/or mounting financial pressure as the country's population ages. Thus, the NBIM fund is not currently paying out sizeable amounts of cash for current consumption.

Chapter 9

1. The Common Agricultural Policy (CAP) is the policy stricture of the European Union that guides agricultural subsidies and programs.

2. The World Trade Organization mission statement can be found at http://www.wto.org/english/thewto_e/whatis_e/wto_dg_stat_e.htm.

3. Namely, New York, Pennsylvania, Ohio, Maryland, West Virginia, New Jersey, Kentucky, and Tennessee.

4. Other producers of uranium include Canada (20 percent), Australia (16 percent), Namibia (8 percent), Russian Federation (7 percent), Niger (6 percent), Uzbekistan (5 percent), United States (3 percent), Ukraine (2 percent), China (2 percent), India (1 percent), South Africa (1 percent), Czech Republic (1 percent), Brazil (1 percent), and Malawi (<1 percent).

5. The UN Environment Program provides leadership on caring for the environment by encouraging nations and individuals to enhance their quality of life in a sustainable way.

Chapter 10

1. This list can be found at found at http://www.worldwater.org/conflict/list/.

2. In September 2011 Tanzania gas reserves estimates were around 10

trillion cubic feet (tcf), and Mozambique's had an estimated 4.5 tcf proven natural gas reserves.

3. The first five-year plan, which was led by Chairman Mao Zedong, ran between 1953 and 1957.

4. For instance, consumers have to pay more for agricultural produce than if they imported food without trade policies and subsidies.

Bibliography

Africa Report, The. http://www.theafricareport.com/.

Alden, Chris. *China in Africa: Partner, Competitor or Hegemon?* London: Zed Books, November 13, 2007.

Arad, Ruth W., and Uzi B. Arad. "Scarce Natural Resources and Potential Conflict." In Sharing Global Resources, edited by Ruth W. Arad, 23–104. New York: McGraw-Hill Book Company, 1979.

Baah Yaw, Anthony, and Herbert Jauch, eds. *Chinese Investments in Africa: A Labour Perspective.* African Labour Research Network, May 2009. http://sask-fi-bin.directo.fi/@Bin/bac4e8c2618871bcbb3ec798c4ee1c34/1325165044/application/pdf/298928/China-Africa%20Report%202009-final.pdf.

Bank of International Settlements. "BIS Quarterly Review," December 2011. http://www.bis.org/publ/qtrpdf/r_qa1112.pdf.

Barrow, John Henry. *The Mirror of Parliament,* vol. 3. London: Longman, Brown, Green & Longmans, 1840.

Bearak, Barry. "Zambia Uneasily Balances Chinese Investment and Workers' Resentment." *New York Times.* November 20, 2010.

Brautigam, Deborah. *Chinese Aid and African Development: Chinese Aid and African Development: Exporting Green Revolution.* New York: St. Martin's Press, 1998.

_____. "Chinese Workers in Africa." China in Africa: The Real Story. http://www.chinaafricarealstory.com/p/chinese-workers-in-africa-anecdotes.html.

Bruinsma, Jelle. "The Resource Outlook to 2050: By How Much Do Land, Water and Crop Yields Need to Increase by 2050?" Paper presented at the FAO Expert Meeting How to Feed the World in 2050, June 24–26, 2009.

Chen, Z., and J. Jian. "Chinese Provinces as Foreign Policy Actors in Africa." Occasional paper no. 22. South African Institute of International Affairs. Johannesburg, 2009.

CLSA. "Global Agriculture: Hungry Planet: Yes, We Can Feed the World." Crédit Agricole Securities. March 2011.

Collier, Paul. "Rebellion as a Quasi-Criminal Activity." *Journal of Conflict Resolution* 44, no. 6 (2000): 839–53.

Collier, Paul, and Anke Hoeffler. "Greed and Grievance in Civil War." World Bank Policy Research Paper 2355. Washington, DC: World Bank, May 2000.

Cotula, L., S. Vermeulen, R. Leonard, and J. Keeley. "Land Grab or Development Opportunity? Agricultural Investment and International Land Deals in Africa." Rome: FAO and IIED, 2009.

"CTIA—The Wireless Association Semi-Annual Survey Reveals Historical Wireless Trend." October 11, 2011. http://www.ctia.org/media/press/body.cfm/prid/2133.

Cuffaro, N. "The Record of FDI in Developing Country Agriculture." Paper presented at the FAO Expert Meeting on Foreign Investment in Developing Country Agriculture, Rome, July 30–31, 2009.

Cui, Shunji, and Ruth Kattumuri. "Cultivated Land Conversion in China and the Potential for Food Security and Sustainability." LSE Asia Research Centre Working Paper 35. http://www2.lse.ac.uk/asiaresearchcentre/_files/arcwp35-cuikattumuri.pdf.

De Soto, Hernando. *The Mystery of Capital: Why Capitalism Triumphs in the West and Fails Everywhere Else.* New York: Basic Books, 2003.

Diamond, Jared M. *Guns, Germs, and Steel: The Fates of Human Societies.* London: Jonathan Cape, 1997.

Dobbs, Richard, and Shirish Sankhe. "Comparing Urbanization in China and India." *McKinsey Quarterly.* http://www.asia.udp.cl/Informes/2010/china_india.pdf.

Downs, Erica. *Inside China, Inc: China Development Bank's Cross-Border Energy Deals.* John L. Thornton China Center, Brookings Institution, March 2011.

Durand, John D. "The Modern Expansion of World Population." Proceedings of the American Philosophical Society, vol. 111, no. 3, *Population Problems* (June 22, 1967): 136–159.

Fearon, James D., and David D. Latin. "Ethnicity, Insurgency, and Civil War." *American Political Science Review* 97, no. 1 (2003): 75–91.

Food and Agricultural Organization. "Assessing the Nature, Extent and Impacts of FDI on West African Agriculture: The Case of Ghana and Senegal." The State of Agricultural Commodity Markets. FAO, Rome, 2009.

_____. "Foreign Direct Investment in Sudan (2000–2008): Magnitude, Location and Allocation." The State of Agricultural Commodity Markets. Rome: FAO, 2009.

_____. "Foreign Investment in the Agricultural Sector: Egypt Case Study." The State of Agricultural Commodity Markets. Rome: FAO, 2009.

_____. "High Food Prices and the Food Crisis—Experiences and Lessons Learned." The State of Agricultural Commodity Markets. Rome: FAO, 2009.

_____. "International Investment in Agricultural Production in Morocco." The State of Agricultural Commodity Markets. Rome: FAO, 2009.

_____. "Statistics." Food and Agriculture Organization of the United Nations. http://www.fao.org/corp/statistics/en/.

Gerlach, A. "Resource-Seeking Foreign Direct Investments in Africa," Rome: FAO, 2010.

Glaeser, Edward L., and Matthew E. Kahn. "The Greenness of Cities: Carbon Dioxide Emissions and Urban Development." *Journal of Urban Economics* 67, no. 3 (May 2010): 404–418.

Gleick, Peter H. "Water and Conflict: Fresh Water Resources and International Security." *International Security* 18, no. 1 (1993): 79–112.

"Global Unease with Major World Powers." Pew Global Attitudes Project. June 27, 2007.

Goldman Sachs, and Jim O'Neill. "Building Better Global Economic BRICs." Global Economics Paper No. 66. Goldman Sachs, 2001.

Goldman Sachs, Jim O'Neill, Sandra Lawson, and Roopa Purushothaman. "The BRICs and Global Markets: Crude, Cars and Capital." Global Economics CEO Confidential, 2004.

Gorton, Gary B., and K. Geert Rouwenhorst. "Facts and Fantasies about Commodity Futures" NBER Working Paper Series, vol. w10595, June 2004.

GTZ. "Foreign Direct Investment in Land in Madagascar." Eschborn: GTZ, 2009.

_____. "Foreign Direct Investment in Land in Mali." Eschborn: GTZ, 2009.

Hall, Kevin, Juen Guo, Michael Dore, and Carsen C. Chow. "The Progressive Increase of Food Waste in America and Its Environmental Impact." *PLoS ONE* 4, no. 11 (2009): e7940. http://www.plosone.org/article/info%3Adoi%2F10.1371%2Fjournal.pone.0007940.

Harrison, Jeff. "Study: Nation Wastes Nearly Half Its Food." *University of Arizona News*. November 18, 2004.

Human Rights Watch. "'You'll Be Fired if You Refuse': Labor Abuses in Zambia's Chinese State-Owned Copper Mines." Human Rights Watch. http://www.hrw.org/sites/default/files/reports/zambia1111ForWebUpload.pdf.

Humphreys, Macartan. "Natural Resources, Conflict and Conflict Resolution." *The Journal of Conflict Resolution* 49, no. 4 (2005): 508–537.

"In Depth: The Top 10 Oil Fields of the Future." *Forbes*. 2010. http://www.forbes.com/2010/01/20/biggest-oil-fields-business-energy-oil-fields_slide_11.html.

Jiang, Julie, and Jonathan Sinton. "Overseas Investments by Chinese National Oil Companies: Assessing the Drivers and Impacts." Information Paper, International Energy Agency. February 2011.

Jintao, Hu. "President Hu Jintao at the Opening of the Third 'China African Cooperation Forum' and Chinese and African Leaders' Summit." Bejing, November 4, 2006.

Jowit, Juliette. "Call to Use Leftovers and Cut Food Waste." *The Observer*. October 28, 2007.

Kaplan, Robert D. "The Coming Anarchy: How Scarcity, Crime, Overpopulation, Tribalism, and Disease Are Rapidly Destroying the Social Fabric of Our Planet." *Atlantic Monthly*. February, 1994.

Kaplan, Robert. *Monsoon: The Indian Ocean and the Future of American Power*. New York: Random House, 2010.

Kaplinsky, R., and M. Morris. "Chinese FDI in Sub-Saharan Africa: Engaging with Large Dragons." *European Journal of Development Research* 21, no. 4 (2009): 551–569.

Keen, David. "The Economic Functions of Violence in Civil War." Adelphi Paper 320. London: International Institute for Strategic Studies, 1998.

Keqiang, Li. "The World Should Not Fear a Growing China." *Financial Times*. January 10, 2011. http://www.ft.com/cms/s/0/64283784-1c23-11e0-9b56-00144feab49a.html#axzz1MR4QgbLE.

Kiggundu, M. N. "A Profile of China's Outward Foreign Direct Investment to

Africa." *Proceedings of the American Society of Business and Behavioral Sciences* 15, no. 1 (2008): 130–144.

Klare, Michael T. "The New Geography of Conflict." *Foreign Affairs* 80, no. 3 (2001): 49–61.

_____. *Resource Wars: The New Landscape of Global Conflict*. New York: Henry Holt, 2002.

Knaup, Horand, and Juliane von Mittelstaedt. "The New Colonialism: Foreign Investors Snap Up African Farmland." *Der Spiegel*. July 30, 2009.

Kreith, Marcia. "Water Inputs in California Food Production." Water Education Foundation, 1991.

Levy, Marion J. Jr. *Levy's Nine Laws for the Disillusionment of the True Liberal*, 5th ed. Princeton, NJ: Princeton University Press, 1981.

Lowi, Miriam R. "Scarce Water, Abundant Oil: Resources and Conflict in the Middle East and North Africa." Paper presented at the annual meeting of the ISA's 49th Annual Convention, Bridging Multiple Divides. Hilton San Francisco, USA, March 26, 2008. http://www.allacademic.com/meta/p251392_index.html.

Malthus, Thomas R. "An Essay on the Principle of Population." London: Printed for J. Johnson, in St. Paul's Church Yard, 1798.

McGreal, Chris. "Thanks China, Now Go Home: Buy-Up of Zambia Revives Old Colonial Fears." *The Guardian*. February 4, 2007. http://www.guardian.co.uk/world/2007/feb/05/china.chrismcgreal.

McGregor, Richard. *The Party: The Secret World of China's Communist Rulers*. New York: Metropolitan Books, 2010.

Meadows, Donella H., Dennis L. Meadows, Jorgen Randers. *The Limits to Growth (1972): A Report for the Club of Rome*. A Potomac Associates Book.

"Do GM Crops Increase Yield?" Monsanto Company. http://www.monsanto.com/newsviews/pages/do-gm-crops-increase-yield.aspx.

Moyo, Dambisa F. *Dead Aid: Why Aid Is Not Working and How There Is a Better Way for Africa*. London: Allen Lane, 2009.

_____. *How the West Was Lost: Fifty Years of Economic Folly and the Stark Choices that Lie Ahead*. London: Penguin, 2011.

Nord, Mark, Alisha Coleman-Jensen, Margaret Andrews, and Steven Carlson. "Household Food Security in the United States, 2009." Economic Research Report No. 108. November 2010.

Parker-Pope, Tara. "From Farm to Fridge to Garbage Can." *New York Times*. November 1, 2010.

Pimentel, David, Laura Westra, and Reed F. Noss, eds. *Ecological Integrity: Integrating Environment, Conservation, and Health.* Washington, DC: Island Press, 2000.

"Population: One Planet, Too Many People?" Institute of Mechanical Engineers. http://www.imeche.org/news/archives/11-01-27/Population_One_Planet_Too_Many_People.aspx.

"Congo Republic Hails Successful Dam Turbine Test." Reuters. January 29, 2010. http://af.reuters.com/article/investingNews/idAFJOE60S0HW 20100129.

Risen, James. "U.S. Identifies Vast Mineral Riches in Afghanistan." *New York Times*. June 13, 2010.

Rogers, Jim. *Hot Commodities: How Anyone Can Invest Profitably in the World's Best Market.* New York: Random House, 2004.

Ross, Michael L. "How Do Natural Resources Influence Civil War?: Evidence from Thirteen Cases." *International Organization* 58, no. 1 (Winter 2004): 35–67.

Sachs, Jeffrey D., and Andrew M. Warner. "Fundamental Resources of Long-Run Growth." *American Economics Review* 87, no. 2 (1997): 184–88.

Schmidhuber, J. J. Bruinsma, and G. Boedeker. "Capital Requirements for Agriculture in Developing Countries to 2050." Paper presented at the FAO Expert Meeting on How to Feed the World in 2050. Rome, June 24–26, 2009.

Smaller, C., and H. Mann. "A Thirst for Distant Lands: Foreign Investment in Agricultural Land and Water." International Institute for Sustainable Development, 2009.

Stuart, Tristram. *Waste: Uncovering the Global Food Scandal.* New York: W. W. Norton and Co., 2009.

"Sudan, Oil, and Human Rights." Human Rights Watch. November 25, 2003. http://www.hrw.org/en/node/12243/section/32.

Sullivan, Daniel E. "Recycled Cell Phones—A Treasure Trove of Valuable Metals." US Geological Survey Fact Sheet. July 2006.

UNCTAD. "World Investment Report 2009: Transnational Corporations, Agricultural Production and Development." Geneva: UNCTAD, 2009.

UN Environment Programme. "From Conflict to Peacebuilding: The Role of

Natural Resources and the Environment." UN Environment Programme, 2009. http://www.unep.org/pdf/pcdmb_policy_01.pdf.

UN Population Fund. "State of the World Population 2007: Unleashing the Potential of Urban Growth." United Nations Population Fund, 2007.

US National Intelligence Council. "Global Trends 2025: A Transformed World." US National Intelligence Council, 2008.

Vermeulen, S., and L. Cotula. "Making the Most of Agricultural Investment: A Survey of Business Models That Provide Opportunities for Smallholders." Rome: FAO and IIED, 2010.

"Water Conflict Chronology List." Pacific Institute. http://www.worldwater.org/conflict/list/.

Wise, Timothy A. "Food Price Volatility: Market Fundamentals and Commodity Speculation." Triple Crisis. January 27, 2011. http://triplecrisis.com/food-price-volatility/.

Wines, Michael. "China Takes a Loss to Get Ahead in the Business of Fresh Water." *New York Times*. October 25, 2011.

World Bank. "Water Resources Management: A Water Policy Paper." Washington, DC: World Bank, 1993.

"World Energy Outlook 2007 Edition." International Energy Agency. http://www.iea.org/weo/2007.asp.

"World Energy Outlook 2008 Edition." http://www.iea.org/weo/2008.asp.

"World Infrastructure Market April 2010." Railway Gazette. April 15, 2010. http://www.railwaygazette.com/news/single-view/view/world-infrastructure-market-april-2010.html.

Index